AAT

INTERACTIVE TEXT

Foundation Unit 4

Supplying Information for Management Control

In this May 2001 edition

- Layout designed to be easier on the eye - and easy to use
- Icons to guide you through a 'fast track' approach if you wish
- Numerous activities throughout the text to reinforce learning
- Thorough reliable updating of material to 1 May 2001

FOR 2001 AND 2002 DEVOLVED ASSESSMENTS

BPP Publishing
May 2001

First edition June 2000
Second edition May 2001

ISBN 0 7517 6505 8 (Previous edition 0 7517 6208 3)

British Library Cataloguing-in-Publication Data
A catalogue record for this book
is available from the British Library

Published by

BPP Publishing Limited
Aldine House, Aldine Place
London W12 8AW

www.bpp.com

Printed in Great Britain by W M Print
45-47 Frederick Street
Walsall
West Midlands
WS2 9NE

We are also grateful to the Lead Body for Accounting for permission to reproduce extracts from the Standards of Competence for Accounting, and to the AAT for permission to reproduce extracts from the mapping and Guidance Notes.

BPP
PUBLISHING

HOW TO USE THIS INTERACTIVE TEXT

Aims of this Interactive Text

To provide the knowledge and practice to help you succeed in devolved assessments for Technician Unit 4 *Supplying Information for Management Control.*

To pass the devolved assessment you need a thorough understanding in all areas covered by the standards of competence.

To tie in with the other components of the BPP Effective Study Package to ensure you have the best possible chance of success.

Interactive Text This covers all you need to know for devolved assessment for Unit 4 *Supplying Information for Management Control.* Icons clearly mark key areas of the text. Numerous activities throughout the text help you practise what you have just learnt.
Devolved Assessment Kit When you have understood and practised the material in the Interactive Text, you will have the knowledge and experience to tackle the Devolved Assessment Kit for Unit 4. This aims to get you through the devolved assessment, whether in the form of the AAT simulation or in the workplace. It contains the AAT's sample simulation for Unit 4 plus other simulations.

Recommended approach to this Interactive Text

- To achieve competence in Unit 7 (and all the other units), you need to be able to do **everything** specified by the standards. Study the text very carefully and do not skip any of it.
- Learning is an **active** process. Do **all** the activities as you work through the text so you can be sure you really understand what you have read.
- After you have covered the material in the Interactive Text, work through the **Devolved Assessment Kit.**
- Before you take the devolved assessment, check that you still remember the material using the following quick revision plan for each chapter.
    - Read through the **chapter learning objectives**. Are there any gaps in your knowledge? If so, study the section again.
    - Read and learn the **key terms**.
    - Look at the **assessment alerts.** These show the sort of things that are likely to come up.
    - Read and learn the **key learning points**, which are a summary of the chapter.
    - Do the **quick quiz** again. If you know what you're doing, it shouldn't take long.

  This approach is only a suggestion. You college may well adapt it to suit your needs.

Remember this is a **practical** course.

- Try to relate the material to your experience in the workplace or any other work experience you may have had.
- Try to make as many links as you can to your study of the other Units at Foundation level.
- Keep this Text - (hopefully) you will find it invaluable in your everyday work too!

Unit 4 Supplying Information for Management Control

This is a new unit that has been introduced in response to demands that Foundation students should be able to supply management with basic management information. The main objectives of this unit are that students should be able to:

- Recognise relevant information
- Code it correctly
- Make comparisons between the actual data for a period and data from previous periods or forecasts

Students should also be able to spot and report obvious errors such as excessive volumes or major differences in the comparisons that they make. The unit is designed to cover the different basic requirements of a variety of organisations, not just manufacturing organisations.

FOUNDATION QUALIFICATION STRUCTURE

The competence-based Education and Training Scheme of the Association of Accounting Technicians is based on an analysis of the work of accounting staff in a wide range of industries and types of organisation. The Standards of Competence for Accounting which students are expected to meet are based on this analysis.

The Standards identify the key purpose of the accounting occupation, which is to operate, maintain and improve systems to record, plan, monitor and report on the financial activities of an organisation, and a number of key roles of the occupation. Each key role is subdivided into units of competence, which are further divided into elements of competences. By successfully completing assessments in specified units of competence, students can gain qualifications at NVQ/SVQ levels 2, 3 and 4, which correspond to the AAT Foundation, Intermediate and Technician stages of competence respectively.

Whether you are competent in a Unit is demonstrated by means of:

- *Either* a Central Assessment (set and marked by AAT assessors)
- *Or* a Devolved Assessment (where competence is judged by an Approved Assessment Centre to whom responsibility for this is devolved)
- Or *both* Central *and* Devolved Assessment

Below we set out the overall structure of the Foundation (NVQ/SVQ Level 2) stage, indicating how competence in each Unit is assessed. In the next section there is more detail about the Devolved Assessment for Unit 4.

All units are assessed by Devolved Assessment, and Unit 3 is also assessed by Central Assessment.

NVQ/SVQ Level 2 - Foundation (All units are mandatory)

Unit of competence	Elements of competence
Unit 1 Recording income and receipts	1.1 Process documents relating to goods and services supplied
	1.2 Receive and record receipts
Unit 2 Making and recording payments	2.1 Process documents relating to goods and services received
	2.2 Prepare authorised payments
	2.3 Make and record payments
Unit 3 Preparing ledger balances and an initial trial balance	3.1 Balance bank transactions
	3.2 Prepare ledger balances and control accounts
	3.3 Draft an initial trial balance
Unit 4 Supplying information for management control	4.1 Code and extract information
	4.2 Provide comparisons on costs and income
Unit 20 Working with information technology	20.1 Input, store and output data
	20.2 Minimise risks to data held on a computer system
Unit 22 Monitor and maintain a healthy safe and secure workplace (ASC)	22.1 Monitor and maintain health and safety within the workplace
	22.2 Monitor and maintain the security of the workplace
Unit 23 Achieving personal effectiveness	23.1 Plan and organise own work
	23.2 Establish and maintain working relationships
	23.3 Maintain accounting files and records

UNIT 4 STANDARDS OF COMPETENCE

The structure of the Standards for Unit 4

The Unit commences with a statement of the **knowledge and understanding** which underpin competence in the Unit's elements.

The Unit of Competence is then divided into **elements of competence** describing activities which the individual should be able to perform.

Each element includes:

(a) **A set of performance criteria.** This defines what constitutes competent performance.

(b) A **range statement.** This defines the situations, contexts, methods etc in which competence should be displayed.

(c) **Evidence requirements.** These state that competence must be demonstrated consistently, over an appropriate time scale with evidence of performance being provided from the appropriate sources.

(d) **Sources of evidence.** These are suggestions of ways in which you can find evidence to demonstrate that competence. These fall under the headings: 'observed performance; work produced by the candidate; authenticated testimonies from relevant witnesses; personal account of competence; other sources of evidence.' They are reproduced in full in our Devolved Assessment Kit for Unit 4.

The elements of competence for Unit 4 *Supplying Information for Management Control* are set out below. Knowledge and understanding required for the unit as a whole are listed first, followed by the performance criteria and range statements for each element. Performance criteria are cross-referenced below to chapters in this Unit 4 *Supplying Information for Management Control* Interactive Text.

Unit 4: Supplying information for management

What is the unit about?

This unit relates to the role of recognising and providing basic management information. This involves information relating to both costs and income and includes the comparison of actual costs and income against the previous period's data, the corresponding period's data and forecast data.

The first element involves recognising cost centres. It should be noted that in some organisations profit centres or investment centres will be used in place of cost centres, and these will differ depending on the organisation. The element also involves recognising elements of costs, coding income and expenditure and identifying and reporting obvious errors, such as the wrong code or excessive volumes. Individuals are required to extract information relating to the three elements of costs: materials, labour and expenses. The element, however, does not specifically relate to manufacturing as materials will include items such as consumables in service industries, and the majority of costs will probably be labour costs in those circumstances.

The second element is concerned with extracting information from a particular source, for example the previous period's data, and comparing that information with actual costs and income, in line with the organisational requirements. The individual is required to report discrepancies between the two in the appropriate format, ensuring confidentiality requirements are adhered to.

Knowledge and understanding

The business environment

- Types of cost centres, including profit centres and investment centres (Element 4.1)
- Costs, including wages, salaries, services and consumables (Element 4.1)

Accounting methods

- Identifying cost centres (Element 4.1)
- The purpose of management information: decision making; planning and control (Element 4.1)
- The make up of gross pay (Element 4.1)
- The relationship and integration of financial and management accounting (Element 4.1)
- Methods of presenting information (Element 4.2)
- Handling confidential information (Element 4.2)
- The role of management information in the organisation (Element 4.2)
- Awareness of the relationship between financial and management accounting (Element 4.2)

The organisation

- Relevant understanding of the organisation's accounting systems and administrative systems and procedures (Elements 4.1 and 4.2)
- The nature of the organisation's business transactions (Elements 4.1 and 4.2)
- The goods and services produced, bought and delivered by the organisation (Element 4.1)
- The cost centres within the organisation (Element 4.1)
- Organisational coding structures (Element 4.1)
- The organisation's confidentiality requirements (Element 4.2)
- House style for presentation of different types of documents (Element 4.2)

Element 4.1 Code and extract information

	Performance criteria	Chapters in this Text
1	Appropriate cost centres and elements of costs are recognised	1 - 4
2	Income and expenditure details are extracted from the relevant sources	2 - 4
3	Income and expenditure are coded correctly	4
4	Any problems in obtaining the necessary information are referred to the appropriate person	4
5	Errors are identified and reported to the appropriate person	4

Range statement

1. Elements of costs: materials; labour; expenses
2. Sources: purchase invoices; sales invoices; policy manual; payroll
3. Information: cost; income; expenditure
4. Errors: wrong codes; excessive volumes; wrong organisation

Element 4.2 Provide comparisons on costs and income

	Performance criteria	Chapters in this Text
1	Information requirements are clarified with the appropriate person	6 - 7
2	Information extracted from a particular source is compared with actual results	6 - 7
3	Discrepancies are identified	6 - 7
4	Comparisons are provided to the appropriate person in the required format	5 - 7
5	Organisational requirements for confidentiality are strictly followed	6

Range statement

1. Information: costs; income
2. Sources: previous period's data; corresponding period's data; forecast data; ledgers
3. Format: letter; memo; e-mail; note; report
4. Confidentiality requirements: sharing of information; storage of documents

ASSESSMENT STRATEGY

This unit is assessed by **devolved assessment**.

Devolved Assessment *(More detail can be found in the Devolved Assessment Kit)*

Devolved assessment is a means of collecting evidence of your ability to carry out practical activities and to **operate effectively in the conditions of the workplace** to the standards required. Evidence may be collected at your place of work or at an Approved Assessment Centre by means of simulations of workplace activity, or by a combination of these methods.

If the Approved Assessment Centre is a **workplace** you may be observed carrying out accounting activities as part of your normal work routine. You should collect documentary evidence of the work you have done, or contributed, in an **accounting portfolio**. Evidence collected in a portfolio can be assessed in addition to observed performance or where it is not possible to assess by observation.

Where the Approved Assessment Centre is a **college or training organisation**, devolved assessment will be by means of a combination of the following.

(a) Documentary evidence of activities carried out at the workplace, collected by you in an **accounting portfolio**

(b) Realistic **simulations** of workplace activities; these simulations may take the form of case studies and in-tray exercises and involve the use of primary documents and reference sources

(c) **Projects and assignments** designed to assess the Standards of Competence

If you are unable to provide workplace evidence, you will be able to complete the assessment requirements by the alternative methods listed above.

Part A

Introduction to management information

1 Introduction to management information

This chapter contains

Learning objectives

On completion of this chapter you will be able to:

- Explain the purpose of management information
- Describe the main sources of cost and management information
- Understand the effect of the organisation on its accounting and reporting systems
- Differentiate management from financial accounting

Knowledge and understanding

- The relationship and integration of financial and management accounting
- The purpose of management information: decision making; planning and control

1 INTRODUCTION

1.1 The main aim of this chapter is to introduce you to the subject of **management information** and in particular to answer the following questions.

- What is management information?
- Why is management information needed?
- How is management information collected?
- How is management information reported?
- What are the main differences between management accounting and financial accounting?

1.2 Let's start by looking at the first question: **What is management information**?

2 WHAT IS MANAGEMENT INFORMATION?

2.1 **Management** is generally thought of as being the people in charge of running a business (managers).

2.2 **Information** is something that is told, knowledge, news or data (facts and figures).

2.3 **Management information** can therefore be described as knowledge, news or data that is told to the people who are in charge of running a business.

2.4 What sort of knowledge or data might the people in charge of running a business wish to be told?

- How much it costs to make a product in their factory.
- How many products the company sold last month.
- How much was spent on wages last year.
- How many staff the company currently employs.

2.5 These are just some of the questions that management might wish to have answers for. Management information can be as follows.

- Financial information (measured in terms of money)
- Non-financial information (not measured in terms of money)

2.6 Good management information has the following qualities.

- **Reliable**. It is important that management have an accurate picture of what is really happening.
- **Timely**. Information should be available in time for decisions to be made.
- **Relevant**. Management information should be relevant to the needs of the organisation and the individual

2.7 So now you know what management information is, let's go on to look at the second question: **why is management information needed**?

3 WHY IS MANAGEMEMENT INFORMATION NEEDED?

3.1 In order to manage their resources, managers in any organisation need to know on a regular basis how their particular department or section is performing. They will also wish to know whether activities are going as planned and whether any problems have arisen. Accounting systems must therefore provide them with **reliable, up-to-date information** which is **relevant** to the **decisions** they have to take.

3.2 Management information has the following purposes.

- **Planning**
- **Control**
- **Decision making**

3.3 **Planning**. Management needs to decide what the objectives of the company are and how they can be achieved. Management information is used to help management **plan** the resources that a business will require and how they will be used.

3.4 **Control**. Once management puts a plan of action into operation, there needs to be some **control** over the business's activities to make sure that they are carrying out the original plans.

3.5 **Decision making**. Management at all levels within an organisation take decisions. Decision making always involves a **choice between alternatives.** It is the role of the management accountant to provide information so that management can reach an informed decision.

3.6 The information required by a manager will vary according to the nature of the organisation and their individual responsibilities. Look at the following examples.

(a) Senior management will usually be interested in the financial statements (balance sheet and profit and loss account), on a monthly basis.

(b) A foreman in a large factory may want a daily output report for every production shift.

(c) A sales manager may want a weekly report of orders achieved by his sales team.

3.7 Management information is used for a wide variety of purposes. We have already mentioned **planning, control** and **decision making**. Management information is also needed for the following.

- Pricing
- Valuing stock
- Assessing profitability
- Deciding on the purchase of capital assets

3.8 In the present business environment where the rate of change is increasing, good management information systems are seen by many as the key to success. Although such systems give a basis for improved management decisions they do not guarantee good management. Poor information, however, is likely to reduce a manager's chances of success.

3.9 We have now looked at why management information is needed. Let's have a look now at **how management information is collected** by an organisation.

KEY TERM

Management information is information supplied to managers for the purpose of planning, control and decision making.

Activity 1.1 **Level: Pre-assessment**

What do you think are the most important features of good management information?

4 HOW IS MANAGEMENT INFORMATION COLLECTED?

4.1 Basic (prime) sources of management information include sales invoices and purchase invoices. These will also provide information for the financial accounts of a company.

4.2 In most organisations, this accounting information will be keyed into a **computer system** and the **coding structure** (also called the **chart of accounts**) for this system should be set up to provide information in the categories required.

4.3 For example, if the organisation is divided into different business units, costs and income must be coded to the correct unit. In a factory which makes different products, raw materials must be coded to the product which uses them. Errors in coding will lead to inaccurate information.

4.4 We will look at the **recording** of income and expenditure in more detail in Chapter 3. In Chapter 4 we will go on to look at how income and expenditure is **coded**.

4.5 Other **sources of information** may include reports from various departments of the organisation.

- Timesheets, employee and wage information from the personnel department
- Goods received notes and stores issue notes from the warehouse
- Price lists (in-house and suppliers)
- The organisation's policy manual (to ensure that consistent procedures are followed)

4.6 Information will be sorted and amalgamated through the **coding structure** so that the reports required by management can be produced. Ways in which information can be collected include the following.

- **Cost centres** (physical locations which use resources, for example a department, a machine).
- **Profit centres,** (sections of the business which use resources and generate income to match against them).
- **Projects,** for example, research projects, activities (for example invoice processing) or other outputs (for example a job for a specific customer).

KEY TERMS

- A **cost centre** is a physical location in the organisation which uses resources (usually a department or section of a department).
- A **cost code** is a 'shorthand' description of a cost using numbers, letters, or a combination of both.

4.7 EXAMPLE: A TYPICAL COMPUTER COST CODE STRUCTURE

An example of the outline for an 8 digit code is shown as follows.

01	**172**	301
Originating department Cost centre or location	Type of cost or income	End product/service Eg project, contract, job service, product

Therefore the code 01172301 will tell us where the cost came from, what type of cost (or income) it was and which end product or service it should be charged to. For example, it could be from factory department 1, wages, chargeable to product 301. We will be looking at coding in more detail in Chapter 4.

Activity 1.2 **Level: Pre-assessment**

What is the purpose of a computer coding structure?

5 HOW IS MANAGEMENT INFORMATION REPORTED?

5.1 You have already seen that management information should be **reliable**, **timely** and **relevant**. **Relevance** in this context means that reports to managers should enable them to manage the resources for which they are responsible, and to give the required level of detail.

5.2 If management information does not contain enough detail, it may fail to highlight problems within the organisation.

On the other hand, too much detail may hide more important information.

5.3 Numbers are often rounded to make reports easier to read, eg money may be expressed to the nearest £100, £1,000 or £10,000 depending on the size of the organisation.

5.4 The **time periods** covered by reports will also vary for different organisations and for different managers within them. Some computer systems allow managers access to information on a **real time basis** and/or to construct their own reports as necessary.

5.5 It is more common for reports to be provided by the accounting department of an organisation every week or month (or any specified period).

5.6 Reporting information requires the active **co-operation** of the following groups.

- **End users**: managers and supervisors
- **The accounts department**: which usually processes the information
- **The information technology department**: which usually sets up and makes changes to the computer system

5.7 Difficulties may arise when these groups **fail to communicate effectively** or when the system itself is **not flexible** enough to respond to changing needs. Information requirements must be clearly specified.

Activity 1.3 **Level: Pre-assessment**

What are the roles of managers and accounting staff in the provision of management information?

5.8 EXAMPLE: MANAGEMENT REPORT

SUMMARY MONTHLY REPORT TO TRUSTEES OF A CHARITY FOR THE HOMELESS

	Fund raising activities	Donations	Interest on investments	Total
	£'000	£'000	£'000	£'000
Income	15.1	9.8	5.4	30.3
Associated costs	2.1	1.0	n/a	3.1
	13.0	8.8	5.4	27.2
Expenditure				
Mobile catering project				6.2
Medical services				2.1
Warm clothing				3.7
Hostel costs				16.0
				28.0
Shortfall for the month				0.8

This type of report is often backed up with appendices. An appendix would give more details of costs and income to help the trustees decide what to do about the shortfall for the month. The charity has spent £800 more than it received in the month under consideration. Individual managers (for fund raising, the catering project, the hostel etc) will need to receive more detailed reports for their own activities.

Management information

5.9 Management information reports might also show the following.

- Comparisons between planned results (budgets) and actual results
- Year-to-date (cumulative information)
- Comparison of company results and competitor results
- Comparison between current year and previous year's results
- The profitability of a product or service or the whole organisation
- The value of stocks of goods that are still held in store at the end of a period

---

Activity 1.4 **Level: Pre-assessment**

What is the purpose of supplying management information?

---

6 MANAGEMENT ACCOUNTING AND FINANCIAL ACCOUNTING

Activity 1.5 **Level: Pre-assessment**

How do you think management accounting differs from financial accounting?

6.1 As you have seen, the purpose of **management accounting** is to provide managers with whatever information they need to help them manage their resources efficiently and take sensible decisions. There are **no externally imposed rules** about how this is done: it depends on the needs of the organisation.

6.2 The purpose of financial accounting is to provide **accurate financial information** for the company accounts, which will be used by both senior management and external parties (for example investors).

6.3 The data used to prepare financial accounts and management accounts are the same. The differences between the financial accounts and the management accounts arise because the data is **analysed in a different way**.

6.4 **Management accounts**

- They are used **internally** for use within a business only
- They are recorded and presented in a way that is decided by management
- They look at **past** data and also **future** data (for planning purposes)
- They are used to help management in **planning**, **control** and **decision making**

- There is no legal requirement to prepare them
- They include both **financial** and **non-financial** information

6.5 **Financial accounts**

- They are used for **external** reporting
- There is a **legal requirement** for limited companies to prepare them
- They are concerned with **past data** only
- They usually only include **financial information**
- They detail the results of an organisation over a **defined period** (usually a year)

6.6 This chapter has provided you with an introduction to management accounting. Section B of this Interactive Text will take a more detailed look at the ways in which income and expenditure is recorded and in particular, we will be looking at the following.

- Types of income and expenditure
- Documentation of income and expenditure
- Coding income and expenditure

Activity 1.6 **Level: Pre-assessment**

Fill in the missing words in the following:

Management information helps managers to plan, ... and make .... It should be relevant, ... and .... In most organisations it is sorted through a computer by using a .... to produce relevant reports. These reports should not be too detailed as this wastes .... and tends to obscure vital .... Communication and co-operation between managers and the .... and .... departments is usually needed for good management information. Management and financial accounts share some information but differ in the external .... which apply to them.

DEVOLVED ASSESSMENT ALERT

When completing assessments, always make sure that you present your tasks neatly - you are much more likely to impress your assessor if you do so.

Key learning points

- The purpose of **management information** is to help managers to manage resources efficiently and effectively and to take decisions.
- Good management information is **reliable, timely** and **relevant** to the organisation and the individual.
- Inaccurate, late or irrelevant management information may reduce an organisation's chance of success.
- There are no external rules governing the format or content of management information, unlike the financial accounts.
- There are many sources of information for management accounting, some of which are shared with financial accounting.
- Computer systems and coding structures help to sort the information into the categories and formats required for both financial and management accounting.
- Producing useful management reports depends on understanding the needs of the end user and the organisation, processing the information appropriately and having the right computer system.

Quick quiz

1 Why do managers need management information?
2 Which three groups of people should co-operate to produce management information?
3 What is meant by 'reliability' in management information?
4 What does the design of management reports depend on?
5 What is the difference between management accounting and cost accounting?
6 Does good management information give a company competitive advantage?
7 What is a cost centre?
8 What is a cost code?
9 What is wrong with giving managers more information than they need?

Answers to quick quiz

1 Managers need management information to help them plan and control their areas of responsibility and to take decisions.
2 Co-operation is needed between managers, accounting staff and IT staff.
3 Reliable management information reflects what is really happening in the organisation.
4 The design of management reports should depend on the needs of the organisation and the individual.
5 Cost accounting is an important part of management accounting but not all of it. Management accounting also deals with non-cost information required by managers.
6 Good management information may give competitive advantage if it is used properly by managers.
7 A cost centre is a physical location which uses resources, eg a department.
8 A cost code describes where a cost came from, what it was and where it went by using numbers and/or letters set out in the computer coding structure.
9 Too much information wastes their time and may make it more likely that important information is overlooked.

Key learning points

- [illegible]
- Good [illegible]
- [illegible]
- [illegible]
- [illegible]
- [illegible]
- [illegible]

Quick quiz

1. [illegible]
2. [illegible]
3. [illegible]
4. [illegible]
5. [illegible]
6. [illegible]
7. What is a [illegible] centre?
8. What is a [illegible]?
9. [illegible]

Answers to quick quiz

1. [illegible]
2. [illegible]
3. [illegible]
4. [illegible]
5. [illegible]
6. [illegible]
7. [illegible]
8. [illegible]
9. [illegible]

Part B

Recording income and expenditure

2 Types of income and expenditure

This chapter contains

Learning objectives

On completion of this chapter you will be able to:

- Recognise the main elements of cost
- Distinguish direct costs from overheads
- Distinguish capital expenditure from other spending
- Recognise cost centres, profit centres and investment centres

Performance criteria

4.1(i) Appropriate cost centres and elements of cost are recognised

Range statement

4.1.1 Elements of costs: materials, labour and expenses

Knowledge and understanding

- Costs, including wages, salaries, services and consumables
- Types of cost centres, including profit centres and investment centres
- Identifying cost centres
- The cost centres within the organisation

1 INTRODUCTION

1.1 The aim of this chapter is to identify the different types of income and expenditure that you need to know about. Most organisations that you will come across are known as **manufacturing** organisations because they **manufacture** (or make) products.

1.2 You might also come across **non-manufacturing** organisations, these are usually known as **service** organisations. Service organisations don't make products, instead they provide a service. For example, a hairdresser is a service organisation that provides a service in the form of haircuts.

1.3 Another non-manufacturing organisation might be a **non-profit making organisation** such as a charity.

1.4 Whatever the organisation, it is likely to have **income** and **expenditure** associated with it. In this chapter we are going to have a look at the different types of income and expenditure that might arise in various organisations.

1.5 The different types of income and expenditure need to be **collected** properly so that the company can extract the information that it needs quickly and easily. We shall finish off this chapter by looking at how information on income and expenditure is collected.

2 MANUFACTURING COSTS

2.1 Cost information is not only recorded for use in management information but also for other purposes. Records must be kept to comply with **external regulations**.

- The Inland Revenue (for income and corporation tax purposes)
- Customs and Excise (for VAT, Value Added Tax purposes)
- The Companies Acts and Accounting Standards (to ensure that the financial accounts meet certain requirements)

The same information will be used internally, but collected and analysed in a different way.

2.2 Analysis of manufacturing costs is made easier by collecting cost information into **cost centres**.

KEY TERM

A **cost centre** is a convenient area, object, person or activity for which costs are separately collected for further analysis.

2.3 For internal information, **manufacturing organisations** usually have the most complicated costs to deal with so we shall start by looking at the costs involved in running a factory. If a factory manager knows how much it costs to turn raw materials into finished goods this will then help him to decide how much the goods should be sold for.

2.4 There are three main **elements of cost**.

- Materials
- Labour
- Expenses

2.5 For manufacturers costs can be divided further.

- **Direct materials** - which form part of the end product
- **Direct labour** - involved directly in making the product
- **Direct expenses** - it is rare for expenses to be directly traceable to the product

2.6 The factory will also have **indirect costs** or **factory overheads** which are not directly traceable to the product but are still part of the cost of making it.

- **Indirect materials** - such as lubricants for machinery
- **Indirect labour** - such as supervisors and maintenance workers
- **Indirect expenses** - such as heating and lighting for the factory

2.7 EXAMPLE: COSTS

Canine Ltd makes dog leads. It buys in leather, thread and metal clips to make them, employs people to operate stitching machines and assemble the finished leads and has various running costs (overheads) for the rented factory space it uses.

Activity 2.1 **Level: Assessment**

Which element of cost would the following items of expenditure at Canine Ltd represent?

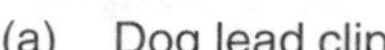

(a) Dog lead clip
(b) Factory rent
(c) Leather
(d) Wages for machine operator
(e) Wages for factory manager

2.8 Costs may also be classified as follows.

- **Variable** - rising and falling with changes in output (like raw materials)
- **Fixed** - remaining the same over large ranges of output (like the rates bill)

2.9 In our example, the amount of leather used would increase if output rose (and decrease if it fell) but the factory rent would not change.

2.10 To calculate the **production cost** of a single dog lead (the **unit cost**), it is quite easy to work out the cost of **direct materials** by taking the amount of leather used (allowing for wastage), multiplying this by the price and adding on the cost of a clip.

2.11 For example, if leather costs £1.50 per metre and clips cost £0.40 each, how much would a 0.5m lead cost?

Cost of leather = £1.50 × 0.5m = £0.75

Therefore, cost of dog lead = £0.75 + £0.40
= £1.15

2.12 **Direct labour** is similar as we can find out how long (on average) it takes employees to stitch and assemble a lead and apply this to their wage rate to find the labour cost per lead.

2.13 The total of direct costs is sometimes called **prime cost.**

	Direct materials
+	Direct labour
+	Direct expenses
	Total direct costs = **prime cost**

2.14 **Factory overheads** (indirect costs) are more complicated to apply to a single production unit because they have to be divided up between the units produced. As you can imagine, this is even harder if the factory makes more than one product, but we need to know how much each product costs to make. **Cost centres** will help us to do this.

2.15 **Production cost centres** are directly involved in production (for example the machining department. Other factory costs are not directly involved in production but must still be taken into account. These costs will be collected into **service cost centres.**

2.16 Examples of service cost centres.

- Maintenance department
- Stores department
- Canteen

2.17 Costs collected in service centres are shared out between the **production cost centres** so that they can be charged to products. The basis for sharing out depends on the type of overhead.

2.18 Examples of how different factory overheads are shared out.

- Factory lighting bill - floor area of department
- Factory canteen costs - number of employees
- Machine maintenance - hours spent in each department

Activity 2.2 **Level: Assessment**

Do you think these costs are direct or indirect, fixed or variable for a manufacturer of baked beans?

(a) Towels for the factory washroom
(b) Labels for the cans
(c) Cleaning materials for the factory
(d) Tomatoes

Activity 2.3 **Level: Assessment**

Match up the following factory overheads with the correct method for sharing out the costs between the different production cost centres.

Factory overhead

Rent of factory
Heating and lighting bills
Insurance of equipment
Personnel office

Method

A = Floor area occupied by each cost centre
B = Cost of equipment
C = Volume of space occupied by each cost centre
D = Number of employees

Helping hand. You should always use your common sense when deciding what the best method to use is for sharing out different factory overheads.

2.19 To summarise what we have learnt so far, production costs for manufacturers are made up as follows.

Direct costs		
Materials	}	Prime costs
Labour	}	
Expenses (uncommon in direct costs)		
Indirect costs		
Materials	}	Manufacturing overheads
Labour	}	
Expenses		
		Total manufacturing costs

2.20 Remember, **direct costs** are traceable to one unit of product, **indirect costs** cannot be traced to one unit of product.

3 OTHER COSTS AND NON-MANUFACTURING ORGANISATIONS

3.1 **Factory costs** are not the end of the cost story because the goods made then have to be **sold. Non-manufacturing organisations** may buy in finished goods and then sell them. This activity is called **trading**. The difference between the income from sales (**sales revenue**) and the **cost of the goods sold** (purchase cost or manufacturing cost as appropriate) is called **gross profit** in the financial accounts.

3.2 Businesses will have other types of costs not directly associated with either making or trading goods. These will include **office** and **administration costs** for the business as a whole. These are known as **non-manufacturing costs**. Examples of non-manufacturing costs are as follows.

- Accountant's salary
- Stationery
- Office rates

3.3 **Non-manufacturing overheads** can also be divided into **labour, materials** and **overheads.**

- The accountant's salary is a non-manufacturing labour cost
- Stationery is a non-manufacturing materials cost
- The office rates are non-manufacturing expenses

3.4 In the financial accounts, these costs will be deducted from **gross profit** in the profit and loss account to arrive at **net profit**. Cost centres may still be used to collect information about expenses. Departments (for example personnel, accounts, training) are often used as a convenient basis for doing this.

3.5 EXAMPLE: ARRIVING AT NET PROFIT

	£'000	£'000
Sales revenue		100
Less cost of goods sold		70
Gross profit		30
Less non-manufacturing costs		
Selling and distribution	12	
Administration	10	
Finance costs	3	
		25
Net profit		5

Activity 2.4 **Level: Assessment**

Do you think the following are direct/indirect factory costs or profit and loss expenses?

(a) Carriage charges on raw materials received
(b) Petrol for delivering goods sold
(c) Electricity bill for the office
(d) A screwdriver for repairing production machines
(e) Factory manager's salary
(f) Finance director's salary
(g) Rates on the office building

3.6 **Service organisations** such as those offering repairs and maintenance (like garages and plumbers), personal services (like hairdressing) or professional services (like solicitors and accountants) make their income without selling physical goods.

3.7 Service organisations still need to collect information. Labour costs are likely to be a very large part of the total costs of providing a service. The costs will be applied to their particular units of output to work out total cost, for example repair garages usually charge for the parts they buy in plus an hourly rate to cover labour and overheads.

3.8 **Non-profit making organisations,** such as charities may include trading activities as well as charitable ones, for example Oxfam. They will need cost information on all their activities for **planning** and **control** purposes and will still use cost centres for collecting information. The cost centres for trading activities will look quite similar to those for commercial organisations, but the charitable activities will probably look quite different.

3.9 In the same way, **public sector organisations** may have a mixture of activities which they charge for (like local authority home helps) and others which are free to users (like medical care within the National Health Service). Public sector organisations will also use cost centres for analysing their costs for different types of activity.

4 CAPITAL EXPENDITURE

4.1 Apart from the running costs of organisations which we have discussed already, most organisations will also spend money on **fixed assets**. Fixed assets are items of **significant value** which are bought for use within the business and not for selling to make a profit.

4.2 Examples of fixed assets

- Land and buildings (except for property companies)
- Machinery (except for manufacturers/suppliers of machinery)
- Vehicles (except for vehicle dealers)

4.3 When an organisation spends money on fixed assets this is called **capital expenditure**.

KEY TERM

Capital expenditure is expenditure on long-term fixed assets which the business intends to retain for its own use.

4.4 There is another cost associated with fixed assets which is known as **depreciation**. Depreciation is the value of the asset which has been used up by the business in any given period.

4.5 As you already know, a car is worth less after a year of use than when it is brand new and an estimate of this **fall in value** (depreciation) is one of the expenses of running the business.

4.6 There are various methods of depreciation and company policy will determine the choice of method for depreciating any particular asset.

4.7 In the **financial accounts**, the original cost of fixed assets will be recorded on the company's **balance sheet** and the depreciation on it will be charged as an **expense** to the **profit and loss account** for each period it is used.

4.8 Low value items may be treated as profit and loss expenses in order to avoid making depreciation charges for such low-value items. Company policy will determine whether an item is depreciated or written off to the profit and loss account in one go. For example, a company may state that all fixed assets that cost less than £2,000 are treated as a profit and loss expense instead of capital expenditure.

4.9 Examples of items which might be charged in total to the profit and loss account in a period are as follows.

- An ashtray for use in the reception area
- A stapler for the office

Activity 2.5 **Level: Assessment**

Do you think the following payments should be classified as capital expenditure, product cost, cost of goods sold or profit and loss expenses?

(a) Overalls for production workers by a manufacturer
(b) Overalls for a retailer of protective clothing
(c) A computer for the personnel manager of an insurance company
(d) A picture for the reception area of a firm of solicitors
(e) Office stationery for a manufacturer
(f) A delivery van for a florist
(g) Timber for a furniture manufacturer
(h) Wages for the commissionaire of a hotel

5 INCOME, PROFIT CENTRES AND INVESTMENT CENTRES

5.1 The most common type of **revenue** (income) comes from selling goods (manufactured or purchased by the business) or from the provision of services. Organisations with more than one product/service, or which cover several geographical areas might want to analyse their income under different categories.

5.2 There may be other types of income for some organisations.

- Grants
- Subsidies
- Sales of redundant fixed assets

Information on these different types of income will usually be collected under separate headings from the organisation's typical revenues for both management and financial accounting purposes.

5.3 **Profit centres**, like cost centres, are used to collect information for further analysis but will include information on both **income** and the **costs** relating to it.

5.4 EXAMPLE: PROFIT CENTRES

A sports centre runs a small cafeteria which is the responsibility of the buildings manager. Separate information is therefore collected about the revenue generated from the cafeteria and the costs of running it. The sports centre does this for the following reasons.

(a) To see whether it is profitable/efficient

(b) To give suitable information to the buildings manager for planning and control purposes

(c) To help decide whether it would be more cost efficient if it were run by contractors

KEY TERM

A **profit centre** is a convenient place for collecting cost and income information for further analysis.

5.5 Profit centre information is needed by managers who are responsible for both revenue and costs.

KEY TERM

Investment centres are used in situations where a manager is responsible for profit in relation to capital invested in his area.

5.6 Managers may or may not have the power to make decisions about capital investment - senior management quite often retains control over decisions on high value investments.

5.7 Many public sector organisations are required to make a particular level of profit related to their fixed assets (**return on capital**). Some commercial organisations also use investment centres.

5.8 Summary

- **Cost centres** collect information on costs
- **Profit centres** collect information on costs, revenues and profits
- **Investment centres** collect information on costs, revenues, profits and profits in relation to the value of fixed assets

Activity 2.6 **Level: Pre-assessment**

Do you think an information system would use cost centres, profit centres or investment centres to provide useful information for the following.

(a) The supervisor of the accounts payable section of the finance department of a large charity.

(b) One of three divisional managers for a trading company.

(c) The personnel manager of a manufacturing company.

(d) A swimming pool manager with authority to buy fixed assets up to £50,000.

(e) The warehouse supervisor for a mail order company.

DEVOLVED ASSESSMENT ALERT

In an assessment, be prepared to complete tasks like the ones in the activities in this chapter.

Key learning points

- The three basic elements of cost are **materials, labour** and **overheads.**
- **Cost centres** are collection points for cost information which needs further analysis.
- Manufacturers collect their factory costs separately to work out their **unit cost** of production.

- Factory costs that are not directly connected with production must be shared out to production cost centres.
- **Gross profit** from selling goods (trading) is found by deducting the cost of goods sold (manufacturing or purchase cost) from sales revenue.
- Other **non-manufacturing costs** are deducted from gross profit to arrive at **net profit**.
- Capital expenditure is not a running cost of a business. Depreciation of capital items is a running cost of a business.
- According to organisational needs, information systems may use **profit centres** (to relate costs to revenues) or **investment centres** (to relate profit to investment in fixed assets) for particular parts of the organisation.

Quick quiz

1 What is the difference between a cost centre and a profit centre?

2 What is a direct cost?

3 What is the difference between production cost centres and service cost centres in a factory?

4 What is gross profit?

5 How do service organisations differ from trading organisations?

6 Is depreciation part of capital expenditure?

7 Why might a charity want to analyse its income as well as its costs?

8 What are the three basic elements of cost?

Answers to quick quiz

1 A profit centre collects information on both costs and revenue but a cost centre only collects cost information.

2 A direct cost can be traced directly to a unit of production.

3 Factory service cost centres are not directly involved in production so their costs must be shared out between production cost centres so they can be charged to production units.

4 Gross profit is the difference between sales revenue and the cost of goods sold.

5 Trading organisations sell goods while service organisations sell services and are likely to have higher labour costs in relation to total costs than traders.

6 No. It is a theoretical cost associated with using the fixed assets of the organisation. Capital expenditure is the actual expenditure on the fixed asset.

7 To separate the different sources of income it might have, such as grants, donations, incomes from trading activities, fund-raising and so on.

8 Materials, labour and overheads.

3 Documentation of income and expenditure

This chapter contains

Learning objectives

On completion of this chapter you will be able to:

- Identify the documents and procedures used for buying and selling
- Identify sources of information on pay
- Understand the bases for allocating expenses and petty cash
- Identify and report errors in documents

Performance criteria

4.1 (ii) Income and expenditure details are extracted from the relevant sources

4.1 (v) Errors are identified and reported to the appropriate person

Range statement

4.1.2 Sources: purchase invoices; sales invoices; policy manual, payroll

Knowledge and understanding

- The make up of gross pay
- The goods and services produced, bought and delivered by the organisation

1 INTRODUCTION

1.1 In the last chapter we looked at the different **types** of income and expenditure that you need to know about for this unit. In this chapter we are going to look at the different **documents** that are used to record this income and expenditure.

1.2 Firstly, we shall consider the documents that are used for buying and selling goods/services.

- Purchase requisition
- Purchase order
- Purchase invoice
- Goods received note
- Sales invoice

1.3 One of the main items of expenditure in service organisations is labour. In all businesses, labour costs need to be recorded and analysed accurately as we shall see as we work through this chapter.

1.4 Finally, some businesses have items of petty cash expenditure. As with purchases and sales of goods and services and labour costs, it is important that smaller items of expenditure such as petty cash are correctly documented.

2 DOCUMENTS FOR BUYING AND SELLING

2.1 The documents involved in buying and selling are prime sources of costs and revenue information. Their number and complexity will depend on the type and size of both the organisation and the purchase. In this section we will look at the typical administrative procedure for the purchase of some desks by a large commercial organisation, Abacus Ltd.

2.2 A **purchase requisition** must be prepared by the person who wants to buy the goods and then it must be countersigned (**authorised**) by the supervisor or departmental head who is responsible for the department's budget.

2.3 The requisition is passed to the buyer (purchasing department) who will find out about suppliers, prices and other details relating to the items that have been requisitioned. If Abacus Ltd has a regular supplier for the goods, then the purchase requisition may show their catalogue number at this stage. Otherwise, it will be filled in later, along with the order number and supplier's name.

PURCHASE REQUISITION

Number: 62
Date 21.02.2001

Quantity	Description	Suppliers Catalogue No	Purchase Order No	Supplier
25	Executive desks	BX 320	489	Desks'r'us

Signed: John Marshall Approved: Jim Davey

Authorised: Mary Great

2.4 If an appropriate supplier is not already used by the buying department then they may send out a **letter of enquiry** to several suppliers in order to find out a price, delivery date, charges, discounts available, and terms of payment, for twenty five desks.

2.5 The different suppliers might respond with a catalogue and a price list (for standard goods), a **quotation** (for non-standard goods) or a letter of reply. For services such as building work or repairs, an **estimate** will usually be provided.

2.6 The buyer must select an appropriate supplier based on the information received. If **discounts** are offered they may be of two types.

(a) A **trade discount** is given for large orders or special customers and will be shown as a deduction on the invoice.

(b) A **cash discount** is usually given for prompt payment within a stated period (for example payment within 7 days gives a 3% discount). It cannot be shown as a deduction until payment has been made.

2.7 If VAT is payable, discounts are deducted from the cost of the goods before the VAT is calculated and added to the invoice.

2.8 Once a supplier has been selected, the buyer will prepare a **purchase order** to ask for the goods to be supplied. Copies of the order are sent to the following.

- The **supplier** - to ask for the goods.
- The **accounts department** - for checking against the invoice when it arrives.
- The **stores section** - for updating the stock records.

- The **goods received** section - so that they expect the goods.

The buyer should also retain a copy on file.

PURCHASE ORDER

Abacus Ltd
4 Smith Street
London
SE11 9JT

Order Number 489
Date: 1.3.2001

Tel: 020 7868 9375

To: Desks'r'us
19 Croydon Road
Balham
CR8 6BZ

Please supply

25 Executive desks Catalogue number Bx320 Price each £200

Delivery by road
To the above address

Signed ....Jim Davey....
(Buyer)

2.9 The supplier will usually send an **advice note** to say when the goods will be delivered and, if delivering the goods with its own transport, a **delivery note** will be sent with the driver for the customer to sign.

2.10 The customer's copy of the delivery note confirms that the goods have been delivered. Another copy of the delivery note is taken by the driver and given to the supplier to confirm that the customer has received the goods. If the supplier does not use its own transport, a **consignment note** will provide the same evidence as the advice note.

2.11 When the desks arrive at the goods received section at Abacus Ltd, a **goods received note** is prepared and sent to other departments so that they know that the goods have arrived. Copies of the goods received note are sent to the following.

- The **accounts department** - to check against the invoice
- The **stores section** - for updating stock records
- The **buyer** - to confirm that the goods ordered have arrived

- The **goods received section** will keep a record on file

2.12 The **supplier's sales department** will send the customer an **invoice** detailing the amounts that they need to pay for the desks. The sales department of Desks'r'us will keep a copy of the sales invoice on file and will send further copies to the following departments.

- **Accounts department** - to record the sale
- **Stores section** - for updating stock records
- **Despatch section** - for delivery of the goods

INVOICE

From: Desks'r'us
19 Croydon Road
Balham
CR8 6BZ

Number: 1340
Date: 10.3.2001

Tel: 020 8775 0679

To: Abacus Ltd
24 Smith Street
London
SE11 9JT

Your order number: 489

Quantity	*Description*	*Price*	£
25	Executive desks Catalogue number BX 320	£200 each	5,000.00
		VAT AT 17.5%	875.00
		Total due	5,875.00

Terms: Payment in 30 days

Delivered on 9.3.2000

2.13 The customer (Abacus Ltd) should check the sales invoice carefully. In particular, they should check the following.

(a) That the goods have been delivered and are in satisfactory condition (check goods received note).

(b) That the price and terms are as agreed (look at the purchase order).

(c) That the calculations on the invoice are correct (including VAT).

2.14 If the sales invoice is correct, it is passed for entry to the purchase ledger. Once it is entered into the purchase ledger it is recorded as a purchase and the invoice is paid. If the sales invoice is thought to be incorrect, the supplier is notified of the discrepancies.

2.15 If the supplier has made any errors on the sales invoice, he will usually issue a credit note (which is effectively the reverse of an invoice). A credit note may be issued for the whole of the invoice, in order to enable both companies to remove it from their books and replace it with a correct invoice.

2.16 If a customer has been overcharged, a **credit note** may be issued to reduce the original sales invoice to its correct value.

If a customer has been undercharged, and the original sales value is too low, the supplier may issue a **debit** note. A debit note is the opposite of a credit note and acts like an additional invoice.

2.17 Not all organisations will go through these steps in their buying and selling procedures but they must all check that goods and services purchased are properly ordered, received and paid for and that sales revenue is properly recorded. Many **computerised accounting systems** will carry out some of these checks automatically.

2.18 The procedures we have described in this section can be summarised as follows.

	CUSTOMER		SUPPLIER
Step 1.	Purchases requisition to tell Buyer what is required		
Step 2.	Enquiry to suppliers	→	
Step 3.		←	Catalogue, quotation, letter of reply
Step 4.	Select supplier and write order	→	
Step 5.		←	Advice note of delivery date
Step 6.		←	Delivery or consignment note to detail goods delivered and signature on delivery
Step 7.		←	Invoice to tell the customer what to pay
Step 8.	Check invoice and make payment		

Activity 3.1 **Level: Pre-assessment**

You work for the accounts department of Abacus Ltd and have received invoice number 1340 from Desks'r'us (see previous paragraphs) for checking.

(a) Does it match the order?
(b) Are the calculations correct?
(c) What else should be checked before passing the invoice for payment?

Activity 3.2 **Level: Assessment**

The goods received note relating to invoice 1340 is shown below.

GOODS RECEIVED NOTE

NUMBER 547

SUPPLIER: Desks'r'us
19 Croydon Road
Balham
CR8 6BZ

Date received: 9.3.2001

Quantity	*Description*	*Order number*
25	Executive desks	489

Carrier	*Received by*	*Checked by*	*Location*
Desks'r'us	M Smith	B Martin	Bay 5

Condition of goods: 1 desktop badly scratched

Distribution:
accounts ✓
stock control
buyer

(a) Should the invoice be paid?
(b) What action should Abacus Ltd take?
(c) Which department(s) in Abacus Ltd should you contact for more information?
(d) What action should Desks'r'us take?

DEVOLVED ASSESSMENT ALERT

The AAT's sample simulation for Unit 4 included a task that required candidates to check a number of invoices. A number of points should be considered when tackling a task like this.

- Is the invoice addressed to the company concerned and not to another company by mistake?
- Have the totals been calculated correctly?
- For purchase invoices in particular, do the items purchased seem to be appropriate for the organisation in question? For example, would a producer of greetings cards be likely to purchase 500 tins of baked beans?

3 WAGES AND SALARIES

3.1 As you have already seen, **labour costs** are an important element of **total costs. Wages** usually refer to weekly payments to employees and **salaries** usually refer to monthly payments. Contractors who work for organisations (for example agency workers or self-employed people) will raise an invoice detailing the number of hours they have worked, and their hourly rate.

3.2 For example, Mr Bloggs is a contract worker for Abacus Ltd. He works in the delivery department and charges the company £7.50 per hour for his services. Last month he worked 125 hours for Abacus Ltd. How much should he invoice Abacus Ltd for the work he did for them last month?

Basic pay = hours worked × hourly rate
= 125 hours × £7.50
= £937.50

3.2 In addition to the **basic payment** for time, **gross pay** may include **other costs**.

- Bonuses
- Commission payments
- Overtime
- Shift allowance
- Output related pay

3.3 Employers must also pay Employer's National Insurance Contributions for employees who earn more than a certain amount. Employers may also make contributions towards employees' pension schemes. Any payments made by an employer make up the gross labour costs.

3.4 Employers also make deductions from wages for employees' compulsory liabilities to other bodies.

- **Income tax** - paid to the Inland Revenue
- **Employees' National Insurance** - paid to the NI Contributions Agency

3.5 Other deductions may be made from an employee's wages by an employer (only when authorised by the employee).

- Employee pension contributions
- SAYE (Save As You Earn Schemes)

- Subscriptions

3.6 Records showing how each individual's pay has been calculated are known as **payslips.** Records of total labour costs which have been analysed in different ways are known as the **payroll.**

3.7 Some workers earn a **flat rate** (they are paid the same amount every week or month) while others are paid an **hourly rate** and may have special **overtime rates.** Workers who are paid hourly often record their hours by using a **clock card** to show the times at which they arrived and left work each day.

3.8 An example of a clockcard is shown below.

Time Sheet No. ....

Employee Name................. Clock Code................. Dept.............

Date................................ Week No. ....

Job No.	Start Time	Finish Time	Qty	Checker	Hrs	Rate	Extension

3.9 Management will be most interested to know how much individual cost and profit centres spent on wages in a particular period. It is important therefore that the total wages for individual employees are collected in the correct cost centres.

3.10 If employees work on different jobs or products that span more than one cost centre, they will need to keep a record of the time spent on each job or product. This can be done by recording wages information on a jobcard such as the one shown below.

JOB CARD

Department ---------------------- Job no ----------------------------

Date -------------------------- Operation no -------------------------

Time allowance ----------------- Time started -----------------------

Time finished -----------------------

Hours on job --------------------

Description of job	Hours	Rate	Cost

Employee no -------------------- Certified by --------------------

Signature ------------------------

3.11 EXAMPLE: SPLITTING WAGES COSTS

A production foreman running two production departments of equal size may have his labour cost split 50 : 50 between them.

A computer programmer serving various departments within the organisation as required may have his labour cost split by reference to the time spent in each department.

3.12 In many **service organisations**, where labour is a very important part of total costs, **charges** to clients will be based upon the hours worked for them. For example, lawyers, accountants and garage mechanics will keep time sheets to show the hours of work done for individual clients and the charge made to the client will have to cover this, plus an amount for overheads.

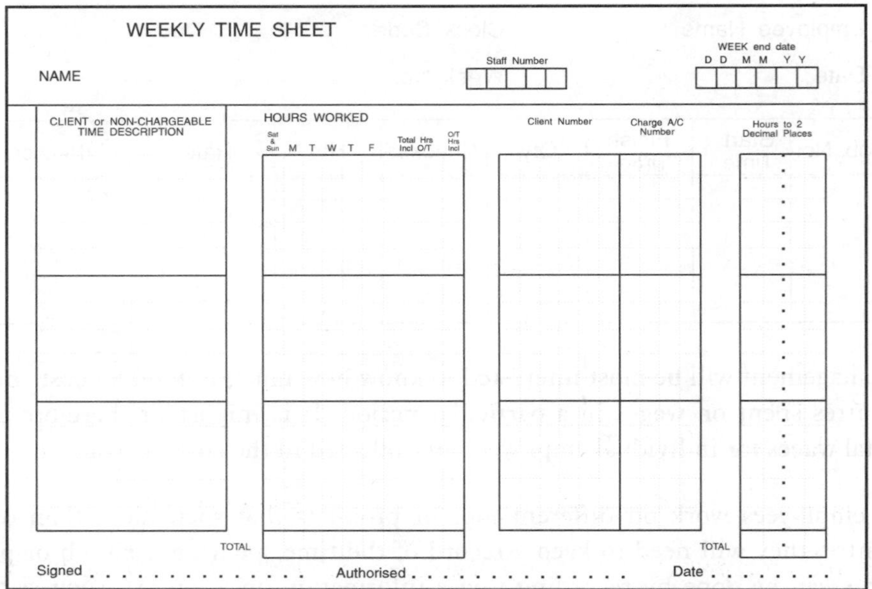

WEEKLY TIME SHEET

NAME | Staff Number | WEEK end date DD MM YY

CLIENT or NON-CHARGEABLE TIME DESCRIPTION	HOURS WORKED Sat & Sun M T W T F	Total Hrs Incl O/T	O/T Hrs Incl	Client Number	Charge A/C Number	Hours to 2 Decimal Places
TOTAL					TOTAL	

Signed . . . . Authorised . . . . Date . . . .

3.13 Employees who agree to work shifts, in particular different shifts over a period time, receive extra wage payments. These extra payments are known as **shift allowances.**

3.14 Sometimes, employees may receive wages that are directly related to the output that they produce, this is known as **output related pay.** For example, workers in a widget factory might receive a basic wage rate plus:

- An extra £100 if they produce more than 1,000 widgets per week
- An extra £150 if they produce more than 1,200 widgets per week

Activity 3.3 **Level: Assessment**

Shown below are two payslips for the month of April for advisers working for a financial services firm, and a corresponding extract from the firm's payroll.

(a) What is the total labour cost to the firm of employing these two advisers for the month?

(b) The firm charges clients on the basis of time spent with advisers. What information will it use to determine this time?

(c) What other costs apart from the adviser's labour cost will be included when working out the charge per hour for clients?

PAY ADVICE

Name: Carol Hathaway   Employee number: 173

Month number: 1   Date: 28.4.2001   Tax Code: 453L

	£	£
Basic pay		1,000.00
Commission		575.00
Total gross pay		1,575.00
Less pension		50.00
Gross taxable pay		1,525.00
Deductions:		
Income tax	233.50	
National Insurance	114.70	
		348.20
Net pay		1,176.80

PAY ADVICE

Name: Mark Greene   Employee number: 174

Month number: 1   Date: 28.4.2001   Tax Code: 490L

	£	£
Basic pay		1,000.00
Commission		450.00
Total gross pay		1,450.00
Less pension		50.00
Gross taxable pay		1,400.00
Deductions:		
Income tax	199.40	
National Insurance	102.20	
		301.60
Net pay		1,098.40

EXTRACT FROM PAYROLL

Employee no	Gross pay	Employee pension	Tax	Employee NI	Net pay	Employer pension	Employer NI
173	1,575.00	50.00	233.50	114.70	1,176.80	50.00	136.49
174	1,450.00	50.00	199.40	102.20	1,098.40	50.00	121.62

Activity 3.4 **Level: Assessment**

You are the Accounts Assistant at Mark Balding's clothes factory (Mark Balding's Ltd).

It is your first day back in the office after a week's holiday. One of the items on your desk is a memo from a cost centre manager and is shown below.

MEMO

To: Accounts Assistant

From: Cost Centre Manager (Denim range)

Date: 9 May 2001

Subject: Missed wage payment

We missed a wage payment for Sandra Bloggs, a sewing machinist (denim range) for the last week of April 2001. Sandra works four days a week and worked 28 hours at the rate of £6 per hour and then worked on her day off (7 hours at time and a half) so that the order for Alma's Ltd was finished by the end of April.

Please calculate the basic wage payments and employee costs and then pass the details on to the payroll department for the personal deductions and coding. Sandra is entitled to an employer's pension contribution of 5% of basic wage payment and employer's national insurance contributions are 12½% above £84 per week.

Many thanks

Task

Complete the wage payment schedule shown below.

PAYROLL CALCULATION SCHEDULE APRIL 2001		
NAME:		
DEPARTMENT:		
BASIC RATE:		
HOURS WORKED:		
HOURS FOR OVERTIME PREMIUM:		
	Calculation	Amount £
BASIC PAY		
OVERTIME PREMIUM		
EMPLOYER'S PENSION CONT		
EMPLOYER'S NIC		

DEVOLVED ASSESSMENT ALERT

The AAT's sample simulation for Unit 4 included a task about wage payments that required candidates to complete the following.

- Calculate hours worked (total)
- Calculate hours of overtime worked
- Perform basic pay calculation
- Perform overtime premium calculation
- Perform employer's pension contribution calculation
- Perform employer's NIC calculation

4 EMPLOYEE EXPENSES

4.1 Some employees will incur expenses when doing their job. These expenses can be reclaimed from their employer. Employee expenses include items such as hotel bills, fares (taxi, train, air and so on), petrol and restaurant bills. In general, expenses which can be reclaimed are those which have been incurred as a result of an employee doing their job.

4.2 **Expense claim forms** are used to check that such claims are valid and also to provide enough detail to ensure that the costs are coded to the correct cost centre. The person making the claim will prepare an expenses claim form. Such forms must be countersigned (authorised) by an authorised member of staff. Receipts must always be attached to the claim form in order to prove that the costs were actually incurred.

EMPLOYEE EXPENSES CLAIM

Name: Susan Lewis **Employee Number:** 137 **Department:** Sales

Date	Details	Petrol	Fares	Hotel	Meals	Other	Total
15/2	Visit DK Smith - Birmingham	25.00			37.50		62.50
21/2	Training conference London		19.50		9.75		29.25
Total		25.00	19.50		47.25		91.75

Signed: S Lewis

Authorised: D Ross Date: 28.3.2001

4.3 Expense claim forms should be checked for the following.

- **Accuracy** - that the arithmetic is right
- **Validity** - that the reason for the claim, method of travel and so on comply with company policy
- **Authorisation** - that the claim has been approved by someone with the power to do so

Activity 3.5 **Level: Pre-assessment**

Look at the example expense claim form on the previous page.

(a) Will any other calculations be needed before entering these figures in the accounts?

(b) Do you think it will make any difference to the coding of the expenses if the person claiming is a saleswoman (visiting a customer and going on a training course) or a training manager (visiting a college and attending a national conference).

5 PETTY CASH

5.1 Most organisations keep some cash available for small items of expenditure, such as taxi fares, coffee, stamps and so on. This is called **petty cash** and will be recorded by using **petty cash vouchers** to make claims. Petty cash expenditure is usually summarised on a **petty cash record sheet**.

PETTY CASH RECORD SHEET FOR MARCH

CASH	DATE	VOUCHER	DETAILS	£ TOTAL	POSTAGE	TAXIS	SUNDRY	VAT
35.00	5/3	37	Registered post	3.40	3.40			
	10/3	38	Taxi	4.50		4.50		
	15/3	39	Dusters	2.00			1.65	0.35
	23/3	40	Taxi	3.50		3.50		
	27/3	41	Stamps	2.60	2.60			
			Month total	16.00	6.00	8.00	1.65	0.35
			Balance	19.00				

5.2 A **petty cash voucher** will show how much was paid out, who received it and what it was for. The person making the claim will prepare the voucher, attach the appropriate receipt to it, sign it and get it countersigned (authorised) by someone in a position of authority before receiving the cash.

5.3 The person in charge of petty cash will make the actual payment and enter the details of all petty cash vouchers onto a **record sheet**. The total expenditure is analysed under various expenditure headings so that the amounts spent on stamps, taxis, coffee and so on in a period is known. These analyses will then be entered into the accounting system.

5.4 At the end of the month the balance (£19) should be left in the petty cash tin. Most organisations will then add an amount to cover what has been spent (£16) so that the next month starts with the same float (£35). This method is sometimes called the **imprest system**.

Activity 3.6 **Level: Pre-assessment**

You are in charge of the petty cash shown above but find only £17.00 in your tin at the end of the month. What do you think could have gone wrong?

DEVOLVED ASSESSMENT ALERT

When completing devolved assessment tasks, always make sure that you think about your own organisation and its accounting systems. Any day-to-day experience that you are able to draw upon will be of great value when completing assessments.

Key learning points

- Companies buying goods and services will use various documents to record and cross-check the process of requisitioning, ordering, receiving and accepting an invoice for the goods and services which they buy.
- Companies selling goods and services will respond to customer enquiries with the information required, advise customers of their delivery date, obtain a receipt for goods delivered and then invoice the customer.
- The documents involved on both sides should help to resolve queries and allow the buyer and the seller to enter the correct information into their accounting and information systems.
- Employee labour costs are made up of wages or salaries plus any additional costs of employment, for example Employers' National Insurance.
- Labour costs may have to be shared between different cost centres.
- Employee expenses reclaimed from employers need to be coded to the right cost centres.
- Petty cash also needs to be coded to the correct cost centres. The summary record sheet provides an analysis of the petty cash expenditure.

Quick quiz

1 How does a customer know when to expect delivery of goods which have been ordered?
2 How does a supplier know that a carrier has delivered goods to their customers?
3 What is the difference between a trade discount and a cash discount?
4 How do discounts affect Value Added Tax?
5 Is Employers' National Insurance deducted from labour cost or added to it?
6 How might labour costs be split between different cost centres?
7 Why are written records needed for employees claiming expenses?
8 What is the difference between a petty cash voucher and a petty cash record sheet?
9 Why will a freelance computer consultant probably keep a time sheet?
10 If your local garage mechanic is paid £8.50 an hour, is this the cost you will expect to see on an invoice for repairs?

Answers to quick quiz

1 The supplier will send an advice note of the delivery date.
2 The supplier should get a signed delivery note from the driver if the supplier's transport is used. If a carrier is used, the supplier should receive a signed consignment note.
3 A trade discount is for particular customers or large orders and will be shown as a deduction on the invoice. A cash discount is for payment made within a given period and therefore cannot be deducted until payment is made.
4 Trade and cash discounts are deducted when calculating Value Added Tax.
5 Employer's National Insurance is an additional labour cost.
6 Labour costs might be split between different cost centres on a proportional basis or on the basis of actual time spent on each.
7 Written records are needed for employee expense claims to make sure that they are valid and to give the information required for coding the expenses correctly.
8 A petty cash voucher gives details of a single cash transaction while the record sheet summarises transactions for an accounting period.
9 Yes. A timesheet will show how much time has been spent on work for clients, administration, and so on. It will also provide a basis for charging clients.
10 No. The invoice will show a higher rate per hour for charging because it must cover overheads and profits as well as the mechanic's wages.

4 Coding income and expenditure

This chapter contains

Learning objectives

On completion of this chapter you will be able to:

- Code income and expenditure correctly
- Identify coding problems
- Report coding problems to the appropriate person
- Appreciate the use of coding for financial and management accounting

Performance criteria

4.1(iii) Income and expenditure are coded correctly

4.1(iv) Any problems in obtaining the necessary information are referred to the appropriate person

4.1(v) Errors are identified and reported to the appropriate person

Range statement

4.1.3 Information: cost; income; expenditure

4.1.4 Errors: wrong codes; excessive volumes; wrong organisation

Knowledge and understanding

- The relationship and integration of financial and management accounting
- Coding structures within the organisation

1 INTRODUCTION

1.1 In many organisations, income and expenditure items are **coded** before they are included in the accounting records. Coded means giving something a **code**. What exactly is a code?

KEY TERM

A **code** is a system of words, letters, figures or symbols used to represent others.

1.2 For example, you have probably all heard of the international code-signal of extreme distress (or help): **SOS**. SOS is a code for 'help'. Businesses also make use of codes in order to make life easier and more organised in the accounts department!

1.3 In this chapter we are going to look at the ways in which organisations use **coding lists** to code items of income and expenditure. We shall also be looking at problems that can occur with **coding systems** and how these problems can be **identified** and **reported** to appropriate members of staff.

2 THE CODING LIST

2.1 Most organisations use computers to record their accounting transactions because they have the following advantages.

- They record and retrieve information quickly and easily
- They are automatically accurate and have built in checking facilities
- They can file a large amount of information in a small space
- They are capable of sorting information in many different ways

2.2 Management information is only one part of the organisation's information system, which will be based on **transaction processing** (data processing). Other applications can be built on top of the basic information system, and spreadsheets can be used in conjunction with it for reporting purposes.

2.3 The information system will also support the needs of the **financial accounts** which, as we have explained are subject to **external regulations.** Under UK company law, directors are responsible for ensuring that accounting records do the following.

- Show an analysis of all income and expenditure
- Show the financial position of the company at any particular moment in time
- Record all assets and liabilities of the company (including stock where applicable)

Accounting records must be retained for future reference.

2.4 Some information must be separately identifiable in order to meet other regulatory requirements (for example **VAT**) or specific accounting requirements (for example **donations** to political causes or charities).

2.5 Some computer systems are able to sort information from transaction processing into the correct categories for both financial and management accounting purposes. This avoids the need to enter data more than once.

2.6 When data is entered into an accounting system, each item is coded with a specific **code** from a list of accounts.

2.7 Codes can be **alphabetical** and/or **numerical**. The length and complexity of a coding system will depend upon the needs and complexity of the organisation.

2.8 For financial accounting purposes it is common to use **general ledger codes** which correspond to the different areas of the balance sheet and profit and loss account.

2.9 EXAMPLE: NUMERIC CODES

Type of account	*Code range*
Fixed asset	1000 - 1999
Current asset	2000 - 2999
Current liability	3000 - 3999
Revenue	4000 - 4999
Long-term liability	5000 - 5999
Capital	6000 - 6999

Within each section, the codes can be broken down into smaller sections

Fixtures and fittings	1000 - 1099
Land and buildings	1100 - 1199
Plant and machinery	1200 - 1299
Motor vehicles	1300 - 1399

and so on. Gaps between the numbers used give scope for breaking the categories down further (for example there could be a separate account for each building) and for adding new categories if necessary.

2.10 Some types of account require **more detail**. For example, each customer needs a separate account, although in the balance sheet the total 'debtors' will be shown. Suppliers (trade creditors) also need an account each and a total for the balance sheet.

2.11 **Alphabetical codes,** using part of the company or person's name, are common but, because names can be duplicated, an additional code may be necessary.

2.12 EXAMPLE: ALPHABETICAL CODES

CUSTOMER	CODE
J MILLER LTD	MIL 010
M MILLER	MIL 015
A MILTON	MIL 025

2.13 Some computer systems save time for operators by offering a '**menu**' of accounts when part of the name is typed in.

2.14 Some codes can help users to **recognise the items** they describe. For example, a shoe shop could code their stock by type of shoe, colour, size, style and male or female. A pair of red women's sandals, size 5, style 19 could then become:

Shoe type	Colour	Size	Style	Male/Female
SA	R	5	19	F
BO	B	8	11	M

and the second item would be brown men's boots, size 8, style 11.

Activity 4.1 **Level: Pre-assessment**

What would code BOR 4 10F stand for?

2.15 We have already stressed the importance of coding costs and revenues correctly for management information (and financial accounting) purposes. The key to achieving this in any organisation is an **understanding** of the coding list and any related guidance in the policy manual.

DEVOLVED ASSESSMENT ALERT

Guidance issued by the AAT states that using your employer's coding documentation to establish codes is one form of workplace evidence for this unit.

3 PRACTICAL CODING

3.1 Depending on the job that you do and the size and type of the organisation that you work for, you may have to deal with coding many different types of transaction or just a limited range. Even if you deal with a limited range, it is useful to have an understanding of the **complete coding structure and the organisation.**

3.2 Imagine that you work for a firm of gardeners and are sitting at your computer looking at a **purchase order** for fertiliser. Firstly you must check this invoice (as we described to you in Chapter 3), secondly, you must enter it into the accounting system, using the principles of double entry. The purchase invoice will create a **creditor** so you need to know how suppliers are coded. It will also be a cost to the firm, but under which category should it be analysed?

3.3 Don't forget that the cost to the company will be the **net** cost and **VAT** will be coded to the **VAT account** to be set off against **VAT on sales**. Coding the net cost will depend on the firm's **policy** for dealing with this type of supply. If the jobs undertaken are mostly large and fertiliser is ordered for particular customers then it will probably be coded so that it can be charged to that **particular job**. If, on the other hand it is delivered to the firm in bulk and used as needed it may well be treated as an **overhead**.

3.4 **Telephone bills** are obviously an overhead cost to the business. Depending on the coding structure and the organisational structure, different telephone lines may be charged to different parts of the business. The individual codes give information for different departments, while the code range for telephone expenses will give a total telephone cost for the organisation.

3.5 In the same way, details of **motor expenses** may be dealt with in one expense account with different accounts for different types of cost.

- Insurance
- Road fund licence
- Petrol
- Repairs and maintenance

3.6 Alternatively details of motor expenses may be analysed by individual vehicles (perhaps using the registration number in the code). In companies with many vehicles, the fleet manager may well want information on costs per vehicle (or type of vehicle) but in small organisations with few vehicles, this may not be necessary.

3.7 Coding structures can also be used to break down various types of **income**. Sales revenue for example can be broken down by different products or geographical areas. If a business charges VAT on sales that it makes, only the **net income** will be coded to the revenue account. The VAT element of any sales will be separately coded to the **VAT account**.

Activity 4.2 — Level: Assessment

Extract from code list

Telephone expenses 5500-5599
5510 General administration
5530 Sales and marketing
5570 Manufacturing

Telephone numbers and locations

020 7668 9923 Managing director
020 7668 9871 Marketing manager
020 7668 9398 Factory floor
020 7668 9879 Accounts office
0879 6534 Salesman's mobile

Which lines would you charge to which code?

Activity 4.3 — Level: Assessment

Here is a summary of the net value of sales invoices for the month of September and an extract from the coding list of a company that sells cosmetics worldwide. Can you apply the right codes to each invoice?

Invoice No	Net sales value £	Country
8730	10,360.00	Canada
8731	12,750.73	Australia
8732	5,640.39	Spain
8733	15,530.10	Northern Ireland

8734	3,765.75	South Africa
8735	8,970.22	Kenya
8736	11,820.45	Italy
8737	7,640.00	France
8738	9,560.60	Australia
8739	16,750.85	Germany

Sales revenue codes: R100 - R199

R110	Area 1	UK
R120	Area 2	North America
R130	Area 3	South America
R140	Area 4	Europe
R150	Area 5	Africa
R160	Area 6	Australia

Helping hand. If you are not sure whether the countries listed are in a particular area of the world - find yourself an atlas and look them up.

Activity 4.4 **Level: Assessment**

An animal charity has various sources of income which are coded as shown below.

DO23	Donations
FR35	Fundraising
GG10	Grants
TR17	Trading

Attach the appropriate codes to the following incomes.

(a) Bequest from the will of a supporter
(b) Sale of animal foodstuffs
(c) Proceeds of the annual dinner dance
(d) RSPCA funding for research into cat sterilisation
(e) Proceeds of annual flag day
(f) Lottery grant for an animal shelter

DEVOLVED ASSESSMENT ALERT

To achieve competence in this unit you should be able to:

(a) Extract information about receipts or payments from purchase or sales invoices or payroll

(b) Code the information you have extracted

4 CODING PROBLEMS

4.1 We have already explained that correct coding requires you to have a good understanding of the **organisation** as well as the **coding list**. You need to know the following.

- The main activities of the organisation
- The main sources of income
- The main items of expenditure
- Details of the organisational structure

In some cases, you may need to ask for **help from other people** in order to code transactions correctly.

Activity 4.5

Level: Assessment

You work for a company which trades in chemicals and also has a small research laboratory. You receive the following invoice.

BOW CHEMICALS
16 Ashton Road
Birmingham
BM11 6HA

Tel 0121-735-9870

To: HA Chemicals
South Street
Godmark
Surrey RH7 8LA

Invoice Number 6135

Your order Number 127

Date: 1.4.2001

Quantity	Description	Price	£
6 litres	Detox FA	£10.90 per litre	65.40
2 bags	Unistat	£15 per bag	30.00
10 drums	Surfactant X	£23 per drum	230.00
15 litres	Dreen	£8 per litre	120.00
		Net total	445.40
		VAT at 17.5%	77.95
		Total due	523.35

Terms: due in 30 days

You need to find out if these items are for resale or use by the research department.

(a) What documents could you look at to help you decide?

(b) Which departments in the company might be able to help you?

(c) You discover that the Detox FA and Unistat are for research purposes and consult the research section of the coding list.

Research expenses R900 - R950

R903	Project 1278
R907	Project 1309
R921	Project 2102

How can you find out which project they are meant for?

(d) Can you think of any procedure which would make your life easier in the future?

Helping hand. Use any knowledge that you have acquired in your place of work - think about what you would do if faced with a similar situation at work.

4.2 An **organisation chart** can help to make sense of the coding structure. Here is a simple one for an accounting firm divided into departments.

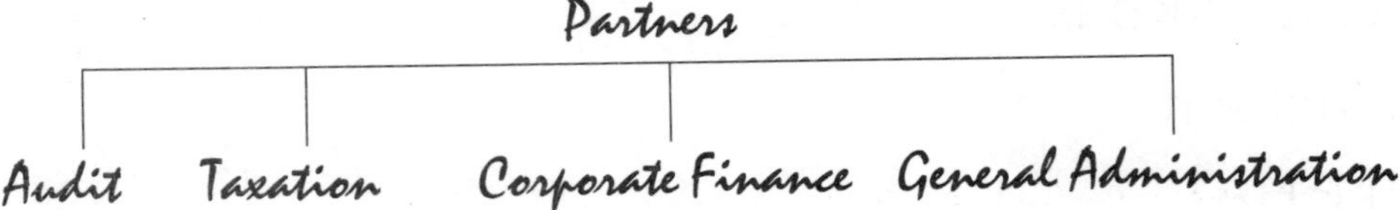

Activity 4.6 — Level: Pre-assessment

Refer to the diagram in Paragraph 4.2 above.

(a) Which department(s) do you think earn income
(b) Which department(s) might have costs shared out to other department(s)?
(c) Which department(s) could not be treated as a profit centre?
(d) Do you think the coding structure will have a single code for revenue?

4.3 Coding errors can happen in a variety of ways, such as errors in keying in the original data and applying the wrong code (because either the transaction or the coding structure have not been understood).

4.4 When management information is produced, large errors are often obvious, for example a doubling of sales revenue in one month is rather unlikely unless there has been a sales campaign in that month. It is more likely that a decimal point has been misplaced in a figure or another form of income has been incorrectly coded to sales revenue.

Activity 4.7 — Level: Assessment

Motor expenses for the three cars belonging to J Miller & Son are all coded to a single expense account and are usually around £1,200 a month. In June the total is almost £15,000. Mr Miller (the firm's owner) asks you to look into the reasons why. You decide to get a print-out of the motor expenses account for June. It looks like this.

Code M057	*Motor expenses*	£
3.6.01	Petrol	22.70
5.6.01	Petrol	18.50
7.6.01	Repairs to S657 PNO	235.70
8.6.01	Petrol	22.00
10.6.01	Petrol	18.00
12.6.01	Tyres for R 393 FGH	140.00
15.6.01	Petrol	24.50
18.6.01	Petrol	230.00
22.6.01	Purchase of T 191 PJF	12,950.00
25.6.01	Petrol	21.50
27.6.01	Petrol	23.65
29.6.01	Road tax R 393 FGH	155.00
30.6.01	Depreciation charge S 657 PNO	290.00
30.6.01	Depreciation charge R 393 FGH	250.00
30.6.01	Depreciation charge T 191 PJF	310.00

Total for the month of June £14,711.55

(a) Can you spot any problems?
(b) What should be done to correct them?

Activity 4.8

Level: Assessment

You are the Accounts Assistant at Mark Balding's clothes factory (Mark Balding's Ltd).

Mark Balding's Ltd makes three ranges of clothes based on different materials.

- Denim Range
- Silk Range
- Lycra Range

Sales at Mark Balding's Ltd are recorded in the following profit centres.

310 UK
320 Europe
330 America (including Canada)
340 Asia (including Australia)

The third digit denotes the type of sale

1 = Denim range
2 = Silk range
3 = Lycra range

Therefore, sale of silk range in America would be coded 332.

Use the coding extract for April 2001 shown below to complete the list of income and expenditure balances at end of April 2001.

CODING EXTRACT
INCOME AND EXPENDITURE
APRIL 2001

Code	**Balance b/fwd 1.4.01**	**Amount coded April 2001**	**Balance at 30.04.01**
	£	£	£
311	23,429	7,220	
312	12,230	3,960	
313	28,930	9,212	
321	27,260	6,250	
322	10,214	2,590	
323	17,928	6,671	
331	46,219	13,652	
332	8,247	2,790	
333	19,715	5,920	
341	24,212	7,262	
342	2,420	659	
343	10,443	3,256	

INCOME AND EXPENDITURE BALANCES YEAR TO DATE APRIL 2001 Sales	Balance at 30.04.01
Denim Range	£
- UK	
- Europe	
- America	
- Asia	
Silk Range	
- UK	
- Europe	
- America	
- Asia	
Lycra Range	
- UK	
- Europe	
- America	
- Asia	

DEVOLVED ASSESSMENT ALERT

The AAT's guidance states that you should be able to spot wrong codes, coding to the wrong organisation and excessive volumes. The sample simulation for this unit assessed candidates on these points.

Key learning points

- A coding list is the key to the information system of an organisation.
- A coding list should be designed so that it is possible to collect information for both management information and financial accounting purposes.
- Coding lists will vary according to the size, type, complexity and structure of an organisation.
- Codes can be alphabetical, numerical or a combination of the two.
- In order to use coding systems correctly you must understand the structure of the codes and the organisation.
- Sometimes, you might need to ask for help from other people in order to assign codes correctly.
- Management information reports should be able to highlight any large items of income or expenditure which have been incorrectly coded.
- Coding errors should be investigated and corrected as soon as possible to ensure that management information and the accounting records are as accurate as possible.

Quick quiz

1 Why do most organisations use computers to record transactions?

2 What is the function of a coding list?

3 Why are gaps often left in the sequence of codes?

4 Is VAT on a purchase invoice treated as a cost?

5 How does the organisational structure of a company affect its coding structure?

6 How might knowledge of the organisation of a company help you to deal with coding problems?

7 Give two causes of coding errors.

8 How do large coding errors usually become apparent?

Answers to quick quiz

1 Because they are faster, more accurate and can store and sort information efficiently.

2 A coding list should enable information to be sorted and extracted in the form required for both management information and financial accounts.

3 Gaps in code sequences allow new accounts to be added easily.

4 No. The net purchase price is the cost to the company. VAT will be coded to the VAT account and can be offset against VAT due on sales.

5 The organisational structure and responsibilities of managers will affect the information a company needs for planning and control. The coding structure should reflect the organisational structure.

6 Knowledge of the organisation can help you to use the coding list more sensibly and to know who you should approach if you require further information.

7 Coding errors are most often caused by errors in keying in codes, insufficient knowledge of the organisation and lack of understanding of the coding list.

8 Large coding errors usually become apparent when management information 'looks wrong'.

Part C

Reporting management information

5 Reporting management information

This chapter contains

Learning objectives

On completion of this chapter you will be able to:

- Clarify information requirements where they are unclear
- Use the appropriate format to present information
- Appreciate legal and other confidentiality requirements

Performance criteria

4.2(i) Information requirements are clarified with the appropriate person

4.2(iv) Comparisons are provided to the appropriate person in the required format

4.2(v) Organisation requirements for confidentiality are strictly followed

Range statement

4.2.3 Format: letter; memo; e-mail; note; report

4.2.4 Confidentiality requirements: sharing of information; storage of documents

Knowledge and understanding

- Methods of presenting information
- Handling confidential information
- Relevant understanding of the organisation's accounting systems and administrative systems and procedures

- The organisation's confidentiality requirements
- House style for presentation of different types of document

1 INTRODUCTION

1.1 In the first four chapters we discussed how you obtain and code management information. In the rest of this Interactive Text we shall discuss what you do with the information you have obtained.

1.2 You can use the information for various purposes. We shall discuss these in the next two chapters. Before then, in this chapter we shall talk about **different means** of communicating information. We shall also discuss when you should not communicate information – when you should keep it confidential.

2 DECIDING WHO NEEDS WHAT

2.1 You learnt in Chapter 1 that management information should be **relevant** to the organisation and the individual.

2.2 The person receiving management information should be able to understand it. Understandability can be helped by:

- Avoiding unexplained technical terms
- Cutting out unnecessary detail
- Using charts, diagrams, tables and good report layouts
- Asking the users' views on required information and presentation

2.3 In many organisations standard reports are issued regularly. The information system may produce the reports directly. Alternatively the reports may need special preparation. They will tell managers responsible for various activities how they are performing. They may be used as a basis for extra rewards such as bonuses, promotions etc.

2.4 Ideally the reports should distinguish between **controllable** and **non-controllable** factors. This is not always easy in practice however.

2.5 Managers may also need **ad hoc** reports to help them with particular problems. For example they may want more detail than is given by the regular reports on a particular aspect of the business. If you have to provide this type of information you must understand **exactly what is required**, including the **format** required for presenting it.

Activity 5.1 **Level: Pre-assessment**

You work for a privatised railway company. You receive a telephone call from the customer relations manager complaining about the regular management reports he receives. 'I have to read six pages to find out if we have overspent our budget and the report doesn't tell me anything else. Please come up with something more useful.'

What questions would you ask as a start to making an improvement?

3 TYPES OF COMMUNICATION

3.1 Choosing the right method of communication is important. We know that many organisations will have standard sets of regular reports in prescribed formats. Many also have a standard **house style** for other documents, that is a particular way of setting things out. This can:

- **Make it easier for employees to read and locate information**
- **Present a consistent image** to people outside the organisation

3.2 If you have to choose which method to use, remember that you communicate most effectively when you use the most suitable method. When choosing, consider the following.

CHOOSING A METHOD OF COMMUNICATION	
Time	How long do you have to prepare the information? How long will it take to send it? How urgent is it?
Complexity	What is the level of detail you need to use?
Distance	How far does the message need to go?
Writing	Is a written record needed as proof or as a reminder? Is the information going to a number of people? Will the information be stored and later retrieved?
Interaction	Do you need instant feedback?
Confidentiality	Which method best guarantees that sensitive information remains confidential?
Recipient	What is the most appropriate way of addressing the recipient?
Cost	Cost must be considered in relation to all the other factors

3.3 As regards **confidentiality**, remember:

- Telephone calls can be overheard.
- Faxed messages can be read by whoever is standing by the fax machine.
- Internal memos may be read by colleagues or internal mail staff.
- Personal letters may be read by the recipient's secretary.

Letters

3.4 You are most likely to use a letter when communicating with someone **outside your organisation.**

3.5 Letters should always be polite, accurate, clear, logical and concise; and should give appropriate references. Spelling and punctuation should, of course, be impeccable!

3.6 EXAMPLE: A LETTER

Brown Bros
24 Croxley Road
Coulton
Surrey
RH3 9BZ

Tel: 0192 730 1933
Fax: 0192 730 1934

Date: 11 May 2001
Our ref: ACF/pj

[Required so that letter can be filed and retrieved]

Your ref: LRS/NP

[Always use this if you have it from previous correspondence]

The Invoice Clerk
Pebble and Sons
16 Rowe Street
Lambourn
Berks
MA6 3AJ

[If possible, address to a specific individual]

Dear Sir,

Re: ....(subject of letter)..................................

[Body of letter]

Yours faithfully

[Yours faithfully goes with 'Dear Sir'. 'Yours sincerely' when writing to a named person (Mr Smith)]

C Ford

(Carol Ford, Accounts Supervisor)

[Type name and title under signature]

Information letters

3.7 For this unit, you need to know about information letters. Other types of letter are covered in Unit 23 *Create and maintain effective working relationships*.

3.8 An information letter is a simple way of presenting a report or details of events or products.

FEATURES OF AN INFORMATION LETTER	
Context	The purpose of the letter with details of when, why and by whom requested, where the information comes from and how obtained
Information requested	Logically grouped and sequenced; volume not excessive
Further action required	Confirm your willingness to be co-operative in providing information, while being firm if you expect information in return

Activity 5.2

Your firm (Brown Bros) has been invoiced by Pebble and Sons for 50 chairs at £25 each when the agreed price was £20. You have spoken to Susan Wade in their sales department, who has asked you to put your complaint in writing. Draft a suitable letter.

Memos

KEY TERM

The **memorandum** or **memo** provides internally the same function as a letter does in communication externally. It can be used for any kind of communication that is best conveyed in writing such as reports, brief messages or notes.

3.9 Memos need less detail than a formal letter.

3.10 EXAMPLE: A MEMO

Forrest Fire Extinguishers Ltd

MEMORANDUM

To: All Staff **Ref:** PANC/mp

From: D B Gavaskar, Managing Director **Date:** 13 January 20X0

Subject: Overtime arrangements for January/February

I would like to remind you that thanks to Pancake Day on and around 12 February, we can expect the usual increased demand for small extinguishers. I am afraid this will involve substantial overtime hours for everyone.

In order to make this as easy as possible, the works canteen will be open all evening for snacks and hot drinks. The works van will also be available in case of transport difficulties late at night.

I realise that this period puts pressure on production and administrative staff alike, but I would appreciate your co-operation in working as many hours of overtime as you feel able.

Copies to: All staff

Main theme

Reason for writing

No need to sign off

Finish by stating clearly what is required of recipient in response

E-mails

3.11 If available, you can use **e-mails** in the same way as a memo, or for external communications where signatures are unnecessary. An e-mail would therefore not be suitable for confirming a contract, but you can use it to respond to a price query.

3.12 E-mail has the following advantages.

- **Speed**. Transmission, being electronic, is almost instantaneous.
- **Economy**. There is no need for stamps etc.
- **Efficiency**. A message is prepared once and sent simultaneously to all addresses.
- **Security**. Access can be restricted by the use of passwords.
- You can request **electronic delivery** and **read receipts**.
- You can use e-mail to **send documents** and **reports** as well as short memos.

Reports

3.13 A formal **report** may be needed where a comprehensive investigation has taken place.

ELEMENTS OF A FORMAL REPORT	
Title	Subject of report
Terms of reference	Clarify what has been requested
Introduction	Who the report is from and to How the information was obtained
Main body	Divided into sections with sub-headings to aid reader Logical order
Conclusions	Summarises findings
Recommendations	Based on information and evidence May be combined with conclusion
Signature	Of writer
Executive summary	Saves time for managers receiving a long report No more than one page

3.14 EXAMPLE: SHORT FORMAL REPORT

REPORT ON DISK STORAGE, SAFETY AND SECURITY

To: M Ployer, Accounts Department Manager
From: M Ployee, Senior Accounts Clerk
Status: Confidential
Date: 3 October 20X8

I INTRODUCTION AND TERMS OF REFERENCE

This report details the findings of an investigation into methods of computer disk storage currently employed at the Head Office of the firm. The report, to include recommendations for the improvement of current procedure, was requested by Mr M Ployer, Accounts Department Manager, on 3 September 20X8. It was prepared by M Ployee, Senior Accounts Clerk, and submitted to Mr Ployer on 3 October 20X8.

II METHOD

In order to evaluate the present procedures and to identify specific shortcomings, the following investigatory procedures were adopted:

1 Interview of all data processing staff
2 Storage and indexing system inspected
3 Computer accessory firm consulted by telephone and catalogues obtained (Appendix I refers)

III FINDINGS

1 **Current system**

(a) Floppy disks are 'backed up' or duplicated irregularly and infrequently.
(b) Back-up disks where they exist are stored in plastic containers in the accounts office, ie in the same room as the disks currently in use.
(c) Disks are frequently left on desk tops during the day and even overnight.

2 **Safety and security risks**

(a) There is no systematic provision for making copies, in the event of loss or damage of disks in use.
(b) There is no provision for separate storage of copies in the event of fire in the accounts office, and no adequate security against fire or damage in the containers used.
(c) There appears to be no awareness of the confidential nature of information on disk, nor of the ease with which disks may be damaged by handling, the spilling of beverages, dust etc.

IV CONCLUSIONS

The principal conclusions drawn from the investigation were that there was insufficient awareness of safety and security among the DP staff, and that there was insufficient formal provision for safety and security procedure.

V RECOMMENDATIONS

In order to rectify the unsatisfactory situation summarised above, the author of the report recommends that consideration be given as a matter of urgency to the following measures:

1 Immediate backing up of all existing disks
2 Drafting of procedures for backing up disks at the end of each day's work
3 Acquisition of a fire-proof safe to be kept in separate office accommodation
4 Communication to all DP staff of the serious risk of loss, theft and damage arising from careless handling of computer disks

M Ployee

Signature

Activity 5.3 **Level: Pre-assessment**

Which method of communication do you think would be suitable for the following?

(a) A complaint to a supplier about the quality of goods supplied
(b) A query to your supervisor on the coding of an invoice
(c) An investigation into the purchasing costs of your company
(d) Notification to customers of a change in the company's telephone number
(e) Reply to an e-mail
(f) Query to the sales department about an expenses claim form

Helping hand. Think about the formality required, the likely length, and whether the correspondence is with an employee of your organisation or an outsider.

DEVOLVED ASSESSMENT ALERT

The range statement for this unit stresses that you should be able to communicate using letters, e-mails, notes and reports.

4 CONFIDENTIALITY

4.1 Keeping some information confidential is an important **legal requirement.** It may also be part of your organisation's **policy**.

4.2 Some requirements are pure common sense. For example most of us would expect details of our wages, salaries, health etc to be kept confidential. Others are less obvious. For example some information about your organisation may be valuable to competitors. This is known as **commercially sensitive information**.

Data Protection Act 1998

4.3 The objective of the Data Protection Act 1998 is to protect individuals from **unauthorised disclosure** of their personal details.

4.4 The Act lays down strict rules about:

- Storage
- Purposes
- Accuracy
- Processing
- Transfer

of personal data.

4.5 The Act applies to information held in any **permanent** form. Therefore it does not matter whether the information is held on paper, on computer or in microfiche or microfilm form.

4.6 The strictest requirements of the Act apply to '**sensitive data**' such as racial origin, health, sexual orientation or political or religious beliefs. The processing of sensitive data is generally forbidden without the consent of the subject.

KEY TERM

Data users are organisations or individuals which use personal data covered by the Act.

4.7 The most obvious use is actually **processing the data**. However use also includes **controlling** the **contents** of **personal data files**.

4.8 Data users must apply to the Data Protection Registrar to be **registered** for holding personal data for a particular purpose. Registered users are only allowed to hold and use personal data for the registered purposes.

KEY TERM

Data subjects are individuals on whom personal data is held.

4.9 Data subjects can **sue** data users for **damage** or **distress** caused by inaccurate data, loss of data or unauthorised disclosure. They also have a legal right to see their own personal data.

Internal requirements

4.10 Within an organisation, the policy manual will often lay down other confidentiality rules. For example some organisations forbid employees to talk to the press without authorisation, or to publish their research results. You can imagine that businesses planning large redundancies or the launch of a new product will not want the information to become public prematurely.

4.11 Paper files with **restricted access** should be

- Listed
- Stored securely
- Only be accessed by specific people

4.12 Computer systems often use **passwords** to restrict access to information that is held on computer. You should never divulge your password to an unauthorised person or keep it in view on your desk. Think of your password as needing as much secrecy as your bank PIN number.

4.13 Use of the **Internet** can pose particular problems in maintaining confidentiality. Many companies have a policy on the purposes for which the Internet should and should not be used. The law surrounding internet information and its protection is still at an early stage of development.

4.14 If you have access to restricted information in any form, you are responsible for protecting it to comply with company policy and the law. You should lock confidential papers or computer disks away when you are not using them. You should not leave them lying around on your desk (or in the photocopier!).

4.15 You should also **not provide confidential information** to **others** outside your department without checking with a supervisor.

Activity 5.4

You receive the following memo

MEMO

To:	Jane Grey (Payroll dept)	Date:	10.6.2001
From:	Alan Jones (Marketing)	Ref:	AJ/ads

Subject: Company advertisement

We want to promote the company's image by using photographs of employees in an advertisement and particularly want to include ethnic minorities to show our commitment to equal opportunities. Please send me a list of all relevant employees showing their department, age and sex.

Draft a suitable reply

Helping hand. Think about whether the data is caught by the Data Protection Act, and if it is, how.

Activity 5.5 **Level: Pre-assessment**

Your company's planning department asks for a copy of the monthly research cost reports for the last six months. Your computer password does not give you access to this information. What should you do?

Activity 5.6 **Level: Assessment**

You are the Accounts Assistant at Mark Balding's clothes factory (Mark Balding's Ltd).

Mark Balding's Ltd makes three ranges of clothes based on different materials.

- Denim Range
- Silk Range
- Lycra Range

Production is organised into the following cost centres with codes as shown.

- Cutting (Cost centre = 810)
- Machining (Cost centre = 820)
- Finishing (Cost centre = 830)
- Packing (Cost centre = 840)

The third digit denotes the type of expenditure.

1 = Materials
2 = Labour
3 = Expenses

Therefore material expense of the cutting department would be coded 811.

An extract of the income and expenditure balance at 30.4.01 for the year ended 31/12/01 are as follows.

INCOME AND EXPENDITURE BALANCES – Y/E 31/12/2001	
Ledger account	**Balance at 30.04.01**
Cutting	£
- Material	20,256
- Labour	21,921
- Expenses	2,960
Machining	
- Material	4,921
- Labour	23,461
- Expenses	3,430
Finishing	
- Material	3,167
- Labour	18,641
- Expenses	4,729
Packing	
- Material	10,694
- Labour	24,999
- Expenses	7,662

Task

Complete the performance report for production cost centres for the year to date 30 April 2001 below and comment on any production cost variances which are more than 10% from budget.

PERFORMANCE REPORT
PRODUCTION COST CENTRES
TOTAL COSTS - APRIL 2001

	YEAR TO DATE 30.04.01	
	Actual £	**Budget** £
Materials		35,000
Labour		85,000
Expenses		15,000

DEVOLVED ASSESSMENT ALERT

The AAT's sample simulation contained a task that was very similar to Activity 5.6 above. It is a good idea to show your workings clearly in an assessment (as we have done above) and make sure you have got a calculator with you so that you can calculate totals easily and quickly.

Key learning points

- Management information should be **relevant to** and **understood** by the individual who receives it.
- **Standard reports** are a regular part of the management information system.
- **Ad-hoc reports** deal with a one-off issue or problem.
- Types of communication include:

  - Letters
  - Memos
  - E-mails
  - Formal reports

  It is important to choose the right one for a given purpose.

- Some information in a company will be **confidential**, either because of the Data Protection Act or because of company policy. Access to it will be restricted.
- If you have access to restricted information, in whatever form, you are responsible for protecting it.
- If in doubt about divulging information **don't** , without referring to a superior.

Quick quiz

1 Why do management reports give limited information?

2 What is the most important thing to ensure before you produce an ad hoc report?

3 Why do some organisations insist on a house style for communications?

4 If you write a letter to 'Dear Mr Thomas', how should you sign it at the end?

5 How does a memo differ from a letter?

6 What is the point of providing an executive summary on a formal report?

7 Why might a personnel department have to be particularly careful about confidentiality?

8 Under what circumstances can data subjects sue data users?

9 Why should companies have a policy on internet use?

10 What should you do with confidential papers?

Answers to quick quiz

1 To avoid swamping the reader with too much detail. Reports should only show what is relevant and necessary to the recipient.

2 Before producing an ad hoc report you must be sure you understand what is required.

3 A house style helps to give a consistent external image and makes it easier for employees to locate information.

4 This letter should be signed 'yours sincerely', followed by a signature, then a printed name and title.

5 A memo is for internal use and can therefore use less detail and be more informal than a letter. Letters are mainly for external use and require details of the sender and recipient plus a more formal tone.

6 An executive summary gives the main points of a report to save time for managers.

7 A personnel department is likely to hold and process personal data within the meaning of the Data Protection Act. It must therefore be registered with the Data Protection Registrar and comply with all the legal requirements as well as company policy.

8 Data subjects can sue data users who have caused them damage or distress by loss of data, inaccurate data or unauthorised disclosure of data.

9 Companies need a policy on Internet use because it is a potential source of breaches of confidentiality.

10 Confidential papers should be locked away unless in use, used discreetly and not copied to unauthorised people without checking with a supervisor.

Part D

Using management information

6 Making comparisons

This chapter contains

Learning objectives

On completion of this chapter you will be able to:

- Explain the reasons for using comparisons
- Understand that different comparisons are used for different purposes
- Describe some bases for financial and non-financial comparisons
- Identify differences between actual results and other data

Performance criteria

4.1(ii) Income and expenditure details are extracted from the relevant sources
4.2(ii) Information extracted from a particular source is compared with actual results
4.2(iii) Discrepancies are identified
4.2(iv) Comparisons are provided to the appropriate person in the required format

Range statement

4.1.2 Sources: purchase invoices; sales invoices; policy manual; payroll
4.2.1 Information: costs; income
4.2.2 Sources: forecast data; ledgers

Knowledge and understanding

- The purpose of management information: decision making; planning and control
- The role of management information in the organisation
- Awareness of the relationship between financial and management accounting
- Relevant understanding of the organisation's accounting systems and administrative systems and procedures

1 INTRODUCTION

1.1 We saw in Chapter 1 that management information helps managers plan, control and make decisions. We have also discussed how managers obtain actual data for the current period.

1.2 This chapter discusses how managers make comparisons between actual data and other data. In doing so they can assess the **significance** of the actual data for the period. Comparing current results with other data can make the information more useful. Comparisons may also help to show up any errors that have occurred.

2 TYPES OF COMPARISON

2.1 Many types of comparison are possible. The ones chosen depend on the needs of the individual and the organisation

2.2 Common comparisons include the following.

Comparisons with previous periods

2.3 The most common comparison of a previous period is when **one year's final figures** are **compared** with the **previous year's**. A business's statutory financial accounts contain comparative figures for the previous year as well as the figures for the actual year. As financial accounts are sent to shareholders, this comparison is obviously of great interest to them.

2.4 Some companies' financial accounts contain figures for the last five years. Comparing the figures for five years may be more valuable than comparing the figures for two years. **Long-term trends** become more apparent over five years. If the comparison is only over two years, one or other year might be unusual for various reasons. This will distort the comparison.

2.5 For management accounting purposes year-on-year comparisons are insufficient by themselves. Management will wish to pick up problems a lot sooner than the end of the financial year. Hence comparisons are often made for management accounting purposes **month-by-month** or **quarter-by-quarter** (three months-by-three months).

Comparisons with corresponding periods

2.6 Making comparisons month-by-month or quarter-by-quarter is most useful when you expect figures to be reasonably even over time. However demand for many products fluctuates **season-by-season**.

2.7 EXAMPLE: SEASONAL FLUCTUATIONS

A company making Christmas decorations had sales for the quarter ended 31 December that were considerably greater than sales for the previous quarter ended 30 September. For the quarter ended the following 31 March its sales decreased significantly again. Should its managers be concerned?

Based on the information given, we cannot tell. All the information tells us is that most people buy Christmas decorations in the three months leading up to

Christmas. Comparing the December quarter's sales with the quarters either side is not very useful, because we are not comparing like with like. People are far more likely to buy Christmas decorations in the December quarter.

A far more meaningful comparison would therefore be to compare the December quarter's sales with those of the December quarter of the previous year, since the demand conditions would be similar.

2.8 This example demonstrates where comparisons with corresponding periods can be very useful, in businesses where the trade is **seasonal** (you would expect significant variations between adjacent periods).

Comparisons with forecasts

2.9 Businesses make forecasts for a number of purposes. A very common type of forecast is a **cash flow forecast.**

2.10 EXAMPLE: CASH FLOW FORECAST

GEORGE LIMITED: CASH FLOW FORECAST FOR FIRST QUARTER

	Jan	*Feb*	*Mar*
	£	£	£
Estimated cash receipts			
From credit customers	14,000	16,500	17,000
From cash sales	3,000	4,000	4,500
Proceeds on disposal of fixed assets	-	2,200	-
Total cash receipts	17,000	22,700	21,500
Estimated cash payments			
To suppliers of goods	8,000	7,800	10,500
To employees (wages)	3,000	3,500	3,500
Purchase of fixed assets	-	12,500	-
Rent and rates	-	-	1,000
Other overheads	1,200	1,200	1,200
Repayment of loan	2,500	-	-
	14,700	25,000	16,200
Net surplus/(deficit) for month	2,300	(2,300)	5,300
Opening cash balance	1,200	3,500	1,200
Closing cash balance	3,500	1,200	6,500

2.11 The purpose of making this forecast is for the business to be able to see how likely it is to have problems **maintaining** a **positive cash balance**. If the cash balance becomes negative, the business will have to obtain a loan or overdraft and have to pay interest costs.

2.12 At the end of the period management will **compare** the **actual figures** with the **forecast figures**, and try and assess why they differ. Differences are likely to be a sign that some of the **assumptions** made when drawing up the original forecast were **incorrect**. Hence management, when making forecasts for future periods, may wish to change the assumptions that are made.

Comparison with budgets

2.13 Most organisations break their long-term goals into:

- **Objectives** (measurable steps towards achieving their goals)
- **Action plans** (detailed steps for achieving their objectives)

2.14 The action plans are often expressed in money and provide:

- An overall view for management
- Assurance that different departments' plans co-ordinate with each other

2.15 The financial plan is usually called a **budget**.

KEY TERM

A **budget** is an organisation's plan for a forthcoming period, expressed in monetary terms.

2.16 You can use budgets to check that the plan is working by **comparing** the **planned results** for the day, week, month or year to date **with** the **actual results.**

2.17 Budgets, like forecasts, represent a view of the future. However the two are not identical. Forecasts represent a prediction of what is **likely to happen,** the most likely scenario. Budgets may be a **target** rather than a prediction. The target may be a very stiff one and it may be far more likely that the business fails to reach the target than that it does achieve the target. However management may feel that setting a stiff target may keep staff 'on their toes'.

2.18 Because comparison of actual data with budgeted data is a very important comparison for management purposes, we shall discuss this aspect in more detail later in this chapter.

Comparisons within organisations

2.19 Organisations may wish to compare the performance of departments and different sales regions.

2.20 EXAMPLE: ANALYSIS OF RESULTS BY SALES AREA

PANDA LIMITED: ANALYSIS OF RESULTS BY SALES AREA

	Area 1	*Area 2*	*Area 3*	*Total*
	£'000	£'000	£'000	£'000
Sales (A)	600	500	150	1,250
Direct costs by areas:				
Cost of goods sold	320	250	60	630
Transport & outside warehousing	60	35	15	110
Regional office expenses	40	45	28	113
Salespeople's expenses	30	25	11	66
Other regional expenses	20	15	8	43
Total direct cost by areas (B)	470	370	122	962
Gross profit (A – B)	130	130	28	288

2.21 Alternatively comparisons may be on a product by product basis.

2.22 EXAMPLE: ANALYSIS OF RESULTS BY PRODUCT

TEDDY LIMITED: ANALYSIS OF RESULTS BY PRODUCT

	Product A	*Product B*	*Product C*	*Total*
	£'000	£'000	£'000	£'000
Sales	200	350	250	800
Variable costs of goods sold	95	175	90	360
Gross contribution	105	175	160	440
Variable marketing costs:				
Transport and warehousing	5	26	37	68
Office expenses	8	20	7	35
Sales salaries	15	44	25	84
Other expenses	2	7	6	15
Total variable marketing costs	30	97	75	202
Contribution	75	78	85	238

2.23 We shall discuss the importance of contribution in the next chapter.

Comparisons with other organisations

2.24 An obvious way of assessing how a business is performing in its chosen market is to **compare** its **results** and **financial position with** its **main competitors**. The main information that will generally be available about its competitors will be the competitor's annual statutory financial accounts. Thus the comparisons are generally made on an annual basis.

2.25 For management purposes comparisons with competitors' positions as shown in the accounts will often give only a broad indication of performance. The information available in statutory accounts is limited. For example the accounts will not give a product by product breakdown of sales, something which would be of great interest to management.

Comparisons with ledgers

2.26 Suppose you receive a query from a customer saying that you have sent him a statement saying that he owes £5,000, when he believes he only owes £1,000. You check the balance he is shown as owing on his account in the sales ledger and indeed it is £5,000. However when you check the invoices that make up that balance, you see that two invoices totalling £4,000 were addressed to another customer, and have been wrongly posted in the sales ledger.

2.27 This example illustrates that you may need to compare the actual data on original documentation such as invoices with data in ledger accounts if **queries arise**.

Non-financial comparisons

2.28 As well as being made in **financial terms** (costs and revenues), you may make comparisons in other ways. For example you may compare units produced or sold. Other possible comparisons include measures of quality/customer satisfaction, time taken for various processes etc.

DEVOLVED ASSESSMENT ALERT

Remember when deciding which comparisons to use, to consider the nature of the organisation, its goals and the activities being reported.

2.29 EXAMPLE: A HOSPITAL CASUALTY DEPARTMENT

A hospital casualty department will aim to deal with incoming patients quickly, efficiently and effectively but numbers and types of patients are hard to predict. Comparing waiting times or cases dealt with per day will be misleading if one day includes the victims of a serious train crash and another covers only minor injuries. Long term comparisons might give a clearer picture and help to identify usage patterns (for example busy Saturday nights). Comparisons with other casualty departments might be even more revealing.

Activity 6.1 **Level: Pre-assessment**

Do you think the comparisons given to the following individuals are the right ones to help assess the performance of their work teams?

(a) Daily output in units compared with same day, previous week for a shift foreman in a car factory

(b) December sales value compared with previous month for the sales manager of a firm trading in Christmas decorations

(c) This year's examination results compared with last year for a secondary school headteacher

Helping hand. Think about the relevance and completeness of the information.

DEVOLVED ASSESSMENT ALERT

The emphasis in this unit is on comparing actual information with other types of information.

3 IDENTIFYING DIFFERENCES

3.1 Differences are only meaningful if they **compare like with like.**

3.2 For example if the heating bill for the summer quarter is less than that for the winter quarter, the difference does not tell you anything about organisational performance, only about the weather.

3.3 If production quantities change from the amount planned or the amount produced in previous periods, then obviously costs will change but by how much? The detailed techniques for dealing with this problem are beyond the scope of this Text. However in essence what you do is **adjust** the figures that you are comparing actual data with to take account of the changed quantities.

3.4 If production is 10% more than it was in the previous period, then we can expect the costs of direct materials to rise by about 10%. The effect on labour costs will depend on whether workers are paid a flat rate or by what they produce. Most factory overheads should not vary with the change in quantities produced.

3.5 Identifying differences only in financial terms may not be very helpful in finding out why they have actually occurred. For example if raw material expenditure is greater than forecast, this could be due to having spent a greater amount or used a greater quantity than planned. In this situation **reporting quantities as well as prices** will be helpful.

Activity 6.2 **Level: Assessment**

Here is part of a sales budget for an ice cream manufacturer.

MONTH	Jan	Feb	Mar	Apr	May	June	Jul	Aug
000 Gallons	1.0	1.0	1.1	1.1	1.2	1.4	1.4	1.5
Sales price £ per gall	8.00	8.00	8.00	8.00	8.00	8.50	8.50	8.50

(a) The sales department complains that they only get information on quantities sold and would like to know what revenue they have earned. They ask you to compare budgeted sales revenue with actual for the last three months (April, May and June). Where would you find the actual sales figures?

(b) You find the figures which are April £9,000, May £10,200 and June £11,800. The sales department telephones you to say that the price rise planned for 1 June was actually brought forward to 1 May.

Produce the report the sales department has asked for and compose a note to go with it, commenting on the effect of the price rise.

4 REPORTING DIFFERENCES

4.1 The main point of reporting differences from the budget is to help managers to take the appropriate action. This makes it vital that they can **understand** the reports they get, ie that the reports are:

- **Relevant to their responsibilities**
- **Not cluttered up with unnecessary detail**

Example of a report

4.2 Here is a production cost report for week 32 for the department making cartons. Output was 5,000 units, as planned. Changes from week 31 have been calculated.

	Week 32	Week 31	Change
	£	£	£
Direct materials			
Cardboard	1,026	1,002	+24
Staples	498	499	-1
Glue	251	249	+2
Ink	99	100	-1
Total direct materials	1,874	1,850	+ 24
Direct labour	825	810	+15
Total direct costs	2,699	2,660	+39
Factory overheads	826	840	-14
TOTAL COST	3,525	3,500	+25

4.3 Some of these changes are very small and perhaps do not need to be shown in detail. An exception report could highlight the changes on cardboard, direct labour and factory overheads.

4.4 Once you have identified important changes, you may need more detail to investigate them.

Activity 6.3 **Level: Assessment**

A ward sister in a private hospital has the following changes in ward costs reported as exceptional.

	Feb	*Mar*	*Variance*
	£	£	£
Nursing salaries	4,500	4,750	+250
Drugs and dressings	237	370	+133

(a) Which of these costs do you think the sister can control?

(b) She decides to investigate the drugs and dressings change and asks you to obtain information on budget, actual this year and actual last year. You obtain the following information from the management accounts and the budget preparation papers.

		Actual last year	*Actual this year*	*Budget*
		£	£	£
January	Drugs	175	182	180
	Dressings	62	72	70
February	Drugs	165	178	180
	Dressings	68	59	70
March	Drugs	170	300	180
	Dressings	60	70	70

Would you look any further and if so, why?

(c) Do you think the drugs and dressings budget should be combined?

Example of comparison of non-financial information

4.5 Here is a report on the conveyancing department of a firm of solicitors for the year 2001.

	Planned	Actual	Last year
Number of conveyances	300	290	295
Number of staff	3	3	2.5
£'000 Fees generated	155	156	145
£'000 Staff costs	62	65	56
£'000 Share of overheads	38	38	35
£'000 Departmental profit	55	53	54

4.6 This shows us that fees earned are well up on last year and better than planned, despite the fact that the number of conveyances are less than planned. Overheads are on target but staff costs are greater than expected.

4.7 Sometimes reports will include information in the form of **ratios or percentages** such as output per employee, profit as a percentage of revenue etc. In the example above, the number of conveyances per employee last year was 118, but this year it is only 96.7. Unless staff are doing more complex work, this needs investigation.

5 COMPARING WITH BUDGETS

5.1 We stated above that budgets can be used to check whether management's action plan is working. You compare the planned results for the day, week, month or year-to-date with actual results. Differences between actual figures and the budget are called **variances**.

KEY TERM

Variance reporting is the reporting of differences between budgeted and actual performance.

5.2 Variances can be:

- **Favourable** if the business has more money as a result
- **Adverse** if the business has less money as a result

5.3 Favourable variances are not always good for the organisation. For example failure to recruit necessary staff will result in a favourable variance (less wages). It may, however, mean that business does not reach its production targets.

5.4 Reporting variances to the appropriate person draws attention to areas which are not running according to plan

Activity 6.4 **Level: Assessment**

Here is an extract from a monthly cost report for a residential care home.

	Budgeted	*Actual*
	£	£
Laundry	1,000	1,045
Heat and light	1,500	1,420
Catering	8,500	8,895
Nursing staff	7,000	6,400
Ancillary staff	10,600	10,950

(a) Calculate the variances for the above items in £ and % terms

(Variance % = $\dfrac{\text{Actual costs} - \text{Budgeted costs}}{\text{Budgeted costs}} \times 100\%$)

(b) If company policy is to report only variances over £500, which would these be?

(c) If company policy is to report variances which are 5% or more of the budgeted amount, which would these be?

5.5 Budgets are also used to allocate financial responsibility to individual managers. For example, the training manager will be responsible for expenditure on training. These responsible people are called **budget holders** and will have to decide what action to take if costs are higher or revenues lower than forecast. Reporting to them is sometimes called **responsibility accounting.**

5.6 The budget process will often document the key results required from budget holders in terms of **quantity** and **quality** as well as money. These targets will clarify how managers at different levels in the hierarchy can contribute to organisational objectives.

	Key objectives
Chief executive	Profit of £5,000 2% growth in market share Improve employee relations
Production manager	No increase in cost per unit 5% increase in units produced 10% reduction in factory labour turnover
Factory foreman	Reduce wastage of materials by 5% Reduce machine downtime by 10% Initiate monthly quality meetings

5.7 This information helps managers to perform their function of **controlling** the organisation. It is like a central heating thermostat with the budget as the temperature setting. Thermostats allow small variations around the setting but if the variation gets larger, they will take appropriate action (switch the boiler on or off) to control the temperature. In the same way, many organisations only report variances over a certain amount to avoid overwhelming managers with unnecessary detail.

KEY TERM

Exception reporting is the reporting only of those variances which exceed a certain amount or %.

5.8 You can classify variances as:

- **Controllable**: can be rectified by managers
- **Non-controllable:** are due to external factors beyond managers' control

5.9 Budget holders may be required to explain why either type of variance has occurred and should take whatever action is needed. If the variance is controllable, management can take action to rectify problems. If the variance is non-controllable, management may wish to revise their plan. Either way budget holders are not necessarily to **blame** for the variance.

5.10 EXAMPLE: COMPARISON WITH BUDGET

A manufacturer of copper pipes has budgeted for £25,000 for copper in month 6 but actual expenditure is £28,000. Possible reasons for this include:

(a) **Price increase** by supplier. This may be controllable. The purchasing officer should try alternative suppliers.

(b) **World price rise** for copper. This is non-controllable. The budget may need revising for the rest of the year.

(c) **Higher factory rejection rate** of finished pipes. This is probably controllable but needs investigation. Is the raw material quality satisfactory? (if not, is this due to supplier, purchasing, warehousing?) Is the factory process at fault? (if so why? Poor supervision? Inadequate training? Machinery wearing out? - find out from the factory supervisors/managers).

5.11 You can see that reporting variances puts managers on the alert but only gives clues as to where the real problems lie.

Activity 6.5 **Level: Pre-assessment**

A hospital decides to cut costs by reducing the number of cleaners employed by 10%. This results in a favourable variance in the budget reports. Is it good for the hospital?

Helping hand. Think of any other impacts a drop in a number of cleaners might have.

5.12 The ways in which managers use budgets is a part of a continuous process of planning, monitoring performance and taking action on variances. This is sometimes called the **control cycle** and is illustrated on the following page.

The control cycle

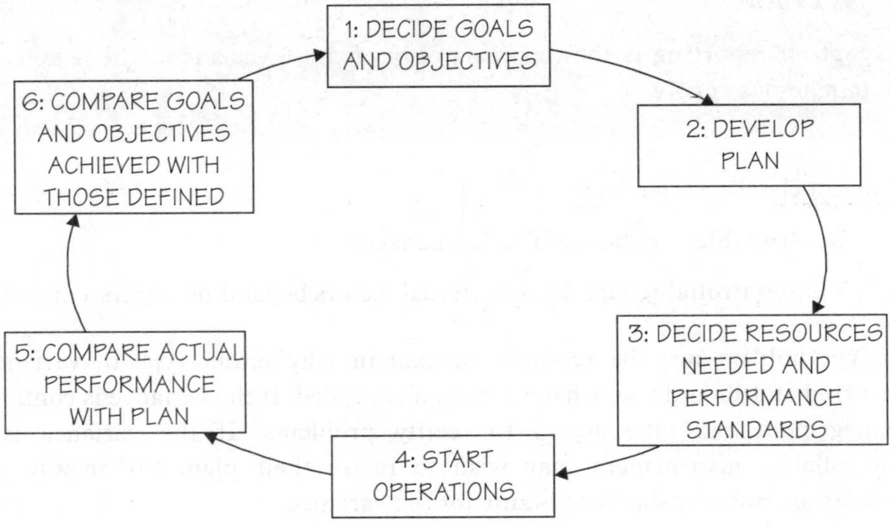

Activity 6.6 **Level: Pre-assessment**

Here is an extract from a sales report for Region 3 month 4 of the budget year (note that YTD stands for year to date, cumulative figures).

		£ actual	*£ budgeted*	*£ actual YTD*	*£ budgeted YTD*
Salesperson	Green	8,500	8,000	35,000	30,000
	Brown	7,600	8,000	25,000	30,000

(a) What are the variances for each salesperson for month 4 and the YTD? Are they adverse or favourable?

(b) Do you think they are controllable?

(c) What action should the sales manager for Region 3 take?

Activity 6.7 **Level: Pre-assessment**

A university librarian believes he exerts excellent management control because he has never overspent his budget and has tightened control over book stocks by reducing the loan period and increasing fines for overdue books. When applying for extra funds for a new book scanning system he is appalled to be told that library usage levels are far too low and that academic staff have resorted to keeping their own stocks of books and videos for loan to students. He suggests that these collections are immediately housed in the library, using staff from the information desk to catalogue and store them.

(a) Are these suggestions sensible?
(b) Is budget performance a good measure of library performance?
(c) What other measures could you suggest?

Other uses of comparisons with budgets

5.13 Businesses obviously need to be **co-ordinated**. For example you cannot increase sales if you do not have the goods available, or increase stocks if you don't have the money to pay for them. Variance reporting is important in alerting management to unplanned changes in one area of the business which may affect another. For example an unplanned decrease in production will affect future sales unless it can be made up.

5.14 In some businesses, comparisons with budgets are used as a basis for extra **rewards** to managers such as bonuses, or profit sharing. This makes the accuracy of forecasting and reporting very important to managers. It may lead to arguments over which costs are controllable by individual budget holders or the way in which fixed overheads are **apportioned** between budget holders.

5.15 Don't forget that **other comparisons** are often used in addition to budget comparisons to assess performance more broadly.

Format of comparisons of budgeted data with actual data

5.16 Your organisation is likely to set a prescribed format. An example is shown below.

5.17 EXAMPLE: MANAGEMENT ACCOUNTS

CARING CROAT LTD: MANAGEMENT ACCOUNTS FOR JUNE

				Budget for year	
	Month (a)	*Budget (b)*	*YTD (c)*	*Year (d)*	*Plan (e)*
	£'000	£'000	£'000	£'000	£'000
Sales	95	100	1,000	2,400	2,800
Cost of sales	48	45	460	1,000	1,000
Gross profit	47	55	540	1,400	1,800
Sales overheads	18	18	175	430	500
Administrative overheads	11	12	101	245	260
Net profit	18	25	264	725	1,040

5.18 Purposes of each column.

- **Month**. These are the actual figures for the month of June.
- **Budget**. The budgeted figures for the month may have been seasonally adjusted or they may be just the total figure for the year, divided by twelve.
- **Year to date**. These are the actual figures for the year up to the end of June.
- **Budget for year**. This is the budgeted figure for the year adjusted for the actual figures to date.
- **Year plan**. This is the original budget for the year.

DEVOLVED ASSESSMENT ALERT

Remember the key elements in presenting comparisons with budget:

(a) Following your organisation's prescribed format
(b) Only highlighting and discussing significant variances

Activity 6.8 **Level: Pre-assessment**

The information below shows budgeted and actual sales for the first six months of the year in money and in units. The sales manager gets a half-yearly bonus if his sales efforts are successful.

	Month	1	2	3	4	5	6	Total YTD
Forecast	Units 000	9.1	10.0	10.2	10.5	10.8	11.2	61.8
	£'000	18.2	20.0	20.4	21.0	21.6	22.4	123.6
Actual	Units 000	9.0	9.9	10.2	10.3	10.6	10.8	60.8
	£'000	18.0	19.8	21.4	21.6	22.3	22.7	125.8

(a) What other department(s) in the business will be directly affected by the results shown?

(b) Should the sales manager receive his bonus?

Activity 6.9

You are the Accounts Assistant at Mark Balding's clothes factory (Mark Balding's Ltd).

As part of your month-end procedures, you have produced the following performance report for production cost centres for April 2001.

PERFORMANCE REPORT PRODUCTION COST CENTRES TOTAL COSTS - APRIL 2001		
	YEAR TO DATE 30.04.01	
	Actual £	**Budget** £
Materials	39,038	35,000
Labour	89,022	85,000
Expenses	18,781	15,000

Mark Balding is concerned that the year to date expenditure at the end of April 2001 is not in line with expected expenditure and has asked you to report on any production cost variances which are more than 10% from budget.

Task

Produce a variance report with comments for Mark Balding.

DEVOLVED ASSESSMENT ALERT

The sample simulation for Unit 4 included a task which required a performance report to be completed and to note any variances more than 10% from budget. This can be calculated as follows.

$$\frac{\text{Variance}}{\text{Budget}} \times 100\%$$

Key learning points

- **Comparing actual results** with **other information** helps to put them in context and may show up errors.

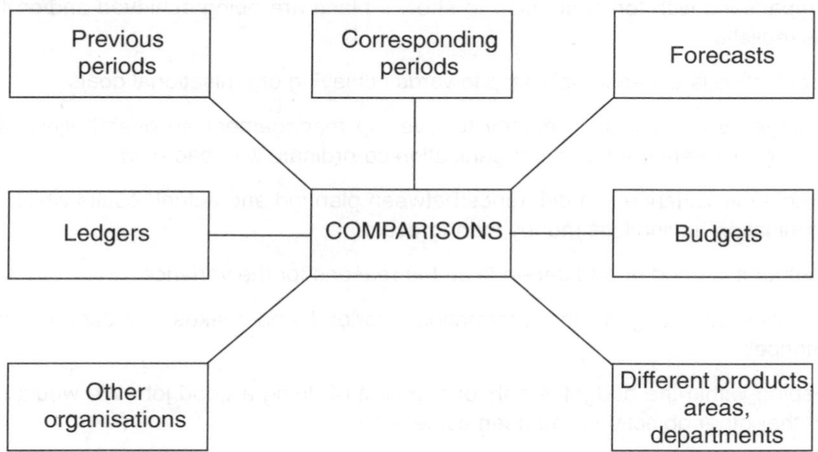

- Comparisons may be **financial** or **non-financial.**
- Choice of the comparison to make depends on the **characteristics** of the organisation, the **individual** and the **activity** being reported.
- When identifying differences you should ensure that you are **comparing like with like.**
- You should report differences in such a way that mangers can **understand them** and pick out **vital information easily**. Comparisons should not be cluttered up with irrelevant information or too much detail.
- Budget comparisons are popular because they show whether budget holders are **achieving** their **targets.**
- Variance reports help budget holders to perform their function of **control.** They are especially useful if they separate controllable from non-controllable variances.
- Variance reports can also alert the organisation to factors which may **harm** the planned **co-ordination** of activities.
- An organisation may use budget reports to determine **extra rewards** for successful managers.
- Budget reports may be **combined** with **other information** such as non-financial information, ratios etc.

Quick quiz

1 Why are comparisons with forecast results useful?
2 What is an objective?
3 Why is a budget expressed in money?
4 What is an adverse variance?
5 Is it good or bad for the organisation?
6 Why is exception reporting popular?
7 Has a budget holder who does not overspend done a good job?
8 Why may managers be given non-financial as well as financial targets?
9 What is a favourable variance?

10 Why do some managers argue about the way in which overheads are shared out?

Answers to quick quiz

1 Comparisons with forecasts help to show if plans are being achieved and/or if the forecast was realistic.

2 An objective is a measurable step towards achieving organisational goals.

3 A budget is expressed in money to give top management an overall view and to ensure plans for different parts of the organisation co-ordinate with each other.

4 An adverse variance is a difference between planned and actual results which results in the organisation having less money than forecast.

5 Whether it is good or bad depends on the reasons for the variance.

6 Exception reporting avoids information overload and makes it easier to spot important variances.

7 Keeping within the budget is only one aspect of doing a good job. We would need to know whether other objectives had been achieved.

8 Non-financial objectives are also important in achieving the organisation's goals and objectives.

9 A favourable variance is one which leaves the organisation with more money than planned, for example a cost lower than expected or revenue higher than expected.

10 Managers might argue because the method of apportioning costs may affect their bonuses, if their bonuses are based on the profits of their department.

7 Using management information for decision making

This chapter contains

Learning objectives

On completion of this chapter you will be able to:

- Use management information to recommend decisions
- Communicate findings appropriately

Performance criteria

4.1 (ii) Income and expenditure details are extracted from the relevant sources

4.2 (iv) Comparisons are provided to the appropriate person in the required format

Range statement

4.2.1 Information: costs; income

4.2.3 Format: letter; memo; e-mail; note; report

Knowledge and understanding

- The purpose of management information: decision making; planning and control
- The role of management information in the organisation

1 INTRODUCTION

1.1 In previous chapters we have covered:

- **Collection** of management information
- **Presentation** of management information
- **Comparisons** with different periods or budgets

1.2 Management information is used for lots of other purposes as well. You will cover some of these in your studies at Intermediate and Technician level, for example valuation of stock and assessment of risk.

1.3 This chapter provides an introduction to general **decision making**, to give you an idea of how management use the information that you provide.

1.4 We also discuss **pricing** which is one of the most important decisions management make. Set your prices too low, and you may not be able to cover costs. Set your prices too high and you may not be able to sell anything.

2 MAKING DECISIONS

2.1 When providing management information for decision making, you must work out which costs and revenues are **relevant** to the decision. If in doubt, always clarify this with the person asking for the information.

2.2 The manager of a factory making two products believes that one of them is much more profitable than the other and asks for a profit statement to compare them.

Profit statement

	Product A	*Product B*	*Total*
	£'000	*£'000*	*£'000*
Sale revenue	100	120	220
Less: Direct (variable) costs	(40)	(70)	(110)
Less: Fixed production overheads	(20)	(20)	(40)
Gross profit	40	30	70
Less: Other fixed expenses	(20)	(40)	(60)
Net profit/(loss)	20	(10)	10

2.3 Do you think the company should stop making product B?

2.4 The important idea here is that products can contribute towards fixed costs provided their:

Sales revenue is greater than variable costs.

2.5 So for example if 1,000 units of a product are sold at £40 per unit and the actual cost of making those units is £25 per unit, then the excess of revenue over costs = 1,000 (40 – 25) = £15,000. This £15,000 is available as a **contribution** to help pay for fixed costs such as insurance.

2.6 The idea of products contributing towards fixed costs is very useful for many decisions. It is called the concept of marginal costing.

KEY TERM

Marginal costing is a system where only variable costs are charged as the cost of sale of an item. Fixed costs are charged to all products as an expense of the period.

2.7 In the example above a **marginal cost statement** would have made it clear that dropping Product B would decrease profits. The statement would look like this.

MARGINAL COST STATEMENT

	Product A	*Product B*	*Total*
	£'000	£'000	£'000
Sale revenue	100	120	220
Less: Variable costs	(40)	(70)	(110)
Contribution to fixed costs	60	50	110
Fixed production costs			(40)
Other fixed costs			(60)
Net profit			10

2.8 In the example, Product B is making a £50,000 contribution to the total fixed costs of £100,000.

Activity 7.1 **Level: Pre-assessment**

(a) Calculate net profit if Product B is dropped and no other action is taken.
(b) What other options could be considered?

Activity 7.2 **Level: Pre-assessment**

Axle Ltd makes canned dog food for supermarkets to sell as 'own brand'. Each can costs 30p in direct materials and labour and sells for 40p. Axle Ltd's fixed costs for next year are estimated at £50,000.

(a) How much does each can contribute towards fixed costs?

(b) How many cans will Axle have to sell next year to cover fixed costs?

(c) If forecast sales are 750,000 cans, what will budgeted profit be?

(d) If these sales leave some spare production capacity in the factory, should Axle accept a special order for 20,000 at 35p per can?

2.9 One way in which management use this information is to assess how safe the business is from making a loss.

KEY TERMS

Breakeven sales is the level of sales where:

Total contribution = Total fixed costs.

At this level the contribution from sales is just enough to cover fixed costs and the company makes neither a profit or a loss.

Margin of safety = $\frac{\text{Budgeted sales} - \text{Breakeven sales}}{\text{Budgeted sales}} \times 100\%$

Margin of safety = $\frac{\text{Actual sales} - \text{Breakeven sales}}{\text{Actual sales}} \times 100\%$

2.10 The calculation of the margin of safety provides a comparison between the sales needed to cover costs and the expected sales. In Activity 7.2 Axle Ltd's breakeven sales are where:

Total contribution = Fixed costs

2.11 Suppose X is the number of units sold needed to break even.

$X\,(0.4 - 0.3) = 50{,}000$

Therefore X = 500,000 units

2.12 As the margin of safety is a percentage, it can either be calculated using units sold or £ sales. Using units sold:

Margin of safety = $\frac{750{,}000 - 500{,}000}{750{,}000} \times 100\% = 33.3\%$

2.13 Put another way the safety volume of sales is 250,000 units. Axle Ltd will have to sell 250,000 less units before making a loss. The safety margin of 33.3% or 1/3 is quite large.

Activity 7.3 **Level: Assessment**

You are asked by the office manager to produce a report on the feasibility of your company installing a drinks vending machine in the office to sell coffee and tea at 30p per cup. At this price, she expects to sell 11,000 cups of tea and 17,000 cups of coffee. The information from the supplier tells you that you can purchase the machine for £2,600 or take a five year lease at £780 per year. An annual maintenance contract is available at £150 a year. The variable cost per cup is 22p for coffee and 20p for tea. Refer to chapter five for advice on report writing and produce a report which includes an assessment of whether income will cover costs, whether purchase or leasing is the best option and any other issues you think are important.

Helping hand. Remember to think about all the costs associated with the machine. What happens when the machine goes wrong?

3 PRICING

3.1 Pricing strategy depends upon two basic factors:

- **Cost**
- **Market conditions**

3.2 Obviously, in the long run the organisation must cover its costs or it will go out of business. Therefore the first step management must take when setting prices is to find out how much it costs to provide the goods or services. Management information systems should contain the necessary information.

3.3 Management must also take into account **market conditions.** The **degree** of **competition** in the market is an important influence. The demand for your product will probably decrease significantly if you increase its price, and make it more expensive than a similar product produced by your main competitor.

3.4 The **pattern of demand** must also be taken into account. As we have seen in previous chapters, the demand for some products varies significantly month-by-month. So for example warm clothing will be priced at full price during the winter. However it is likely to be sold off cheaply during the warmer weather of the spring and summer.

3.5 The **strategy** of the business setting the price is another important influence on pricing. For example, a firm trying to enter a new market with well-established competitors will probably have to undercut their price to gain customers from the competition. However a firm with very little competition will have less pressure to drive prices down. For instance the only plumber within a twenty-mile radius will be able to charge high prices.

3.6 More can generally be sold at a lower price than at a higher one. However firms may not necessarily make the biggest profits by reducing prices. Firms may find it more profitable to have lower sales at a higher price, and therefore higher profit per unit. This will depend on how sensitive **market demand** is to price changes.

3.7 Management information for pricing must therefore include **external information** about demand, competition, market price etc as well as internal cost information.

Activity 7.4 **Level: Assessment**

Bottleo Ltd makes a corkscrew which sells for £5. Budgeted sales this year are 20,000 units at a variable cost of £2.20 and fixed cost per unit of £1.80. Management want to increase profits and have asked the sales manager to research the likely effects of changes in selling price. His forecast is:

Selling price per unit £	*Sales volume* (units)
4.00	29,000
4.50	25,000
5.00	20,000
5.50	17,000
6.00	15,000

He has added a note that if an extra £6,000 is spent on advertising, all these sales forecasts can be increased by 10%.

What would you advise management to do?

Helping hand. Remember the importance of total contribution. How relevant are fixed costs?

DEVOLVED ASSESSMENT ALERT

Decision making is highlighted as an important purpose of management information in this unit.

Key learning points

- Management use management information to help them make a variety of business decisions.
- You will always need know what information is relevant to the decision being made.
- **Marginal costing**, that is assessing the **contribution** which units sold make towards fixed cost, is one useful technique for assessing options for action.
- Pricing decisions depend on **information** about the **market** as well as **cost information.**
- Pricing decisions also depend on **company strategy**.

Quick quiz

1 If a firm reduced production its .... costs will go down but its .... costs will remain the same.

2 If a firm increases production the cost per unit will usually increase/decrease/stay the same.

3 A business will break even when total .... equals fixed costs.

4 What is the margin of safety?

5 Pricing decisions require information on costs and ....

6 What will ultimately happen to a business if the selling price of its product is less than the cost of making it?

Answers to quick quiz

1 If a firm reduced production its **variable** costs will go down but its **fixed** costs will remain the same.

2 If a firm increases production the cost per unit will usually **decrease**.

3 A business will break even when total **contribution** equals fixed costs.

4 The margin of safety is the difference between break even point and forecast or actual sales.

5 Pricing decisions require information on costs and **market conditions**.

6 If selling price is below cost, eventually the business will become insolvent.

Answers to activities

Answers to Chapter 1 activities

Activity 1.1

Good management information is reliable, timely and relevant and will give a manager what he or she needs as a basis to plan, control and take decisions.

Activity 1.2

The purpose of a computer coding structure is to allow information to be sorted and grouped for management information and financial accounting purposes.

Activity 1.3

Managers must be able to specify clearly what information they want, while accounting staff must ensure that data is processed accurately and consistently. Both will need to co-operate with IT staff.

Activity 1.4

The purpose of supplying management information is to help managers manage by monitoring activities, identifying problems and giving a basis for decision making.

Activity 1.5

Management accounting is for internal use and has no set rules on layout or content. Financial accounting is for external as well as internal use and must comply with various external regulations and standards.

Activity 1.6

Helping hand. Remember to fill in *all* of the missing words!

Management information helps managers to plan, control and make decisions. It should be relevant, **reliable** and **timely**. In most organisations it is sorted through a computer by using a **coding structure** to produce relevant reports. These reports should not be too detailed as this wastes **time** and tends to obscure vital information. Communication and co-operation between managers and the **information technology** and **accounting** departments is usually needed for good management information. Management and financial accounts share some information but differ in the external requirements which apply to them.

Answers to Chapter 2 activities

Activity 2.1

Helping hand. First you need to decide whether the items are materials, labour or expenses. Then you need to decide whether they are directly traceable to the product or not.

(a) Direct material
(b) Indirect expense (factory overhead)
(c) Direct material
(d) Direct labour
(e) Indirect labour (factory overhead)

Activity 2.2

Helping hand. Variable costs rise and fall as output rises or falls. Fixed costs usually stay the same as output rises or falls.

(a) Indirect materials (factory overhead) fixed cost
(b) Direct materials variable cost
(c) Indirect materials (factory overhead) fixed cost
(d) Direct materials variable cost

Activity 2.3

Factory overhead	**Method**
Rent of factory	A
Heating and lighting bills	C
Insurance of equipment	B
Personnel office	D

Method

A = floor area occupied by each cost centre
B = cost of equipment
C = volume of space occupied by each cost centre
D = number of employees

Helping hand. You should always use your common sense when deciding which is the best method to use for sharing out different factory overheads.

Activity 2.4

(a) Part of direct factory materials cost
(b) Profit and loss expense
(c) Profit and loss expense
(d) Indirect materials (factory overhead)
(e) Indirect labour (factory overhead)
(f) Profit and loss expense
(g) Profit and loss expense

Activity 2.5

Helping hand. Capital expenditure is expenditure on long-term fixed assets which the business intends to retain for its own use.

(a) Production cost (indirect materials)

(b) Cost of goods sold (presuming they are for sale and not for use in the shop)

(c) Capital expenditure (not for sale and will last for some time)

(d) This depends on how expensive it is. If the value is low then it will be treated as a profit and loss expense but if it is very high (not likely in this situation) it will be treated as capital expenditure.

(e) Profit and loss expense

(f) Capital expenditure

(g) Production cost (direct materials)

(h) Profit and loss expense

Activity 2.6

(a) Cost centre. This person will have no control over revenue.

(b) Profit centre. This person will be responsible for revenue as well as costs for the division. If there were control over capital expenditure too, investment centres might be used.

(c) Cost centre. The personnel department does not earn revenue.

(d) Investment centre. Responsibility will be for costs, revenues and capital expenditure.

(e) Cost centres. This person cannot control revenue.

Answers to Chapter 3 activities

Activity 3.1

Helping hand. Make sure you've got a calculator handy so you can check the sales invoice calculations.

(a) Yes it does match the order.

(b) Yes, the calculations are correct.

(c) The goods received note should be checked to see that goods have been delivered in good condition.

Activity 3.2

(a) No, the invoice should not be paid because one desk was damaged.

(b) Abacus Ltd should inform the supplier and return the damaged desk for replacement so that a credit note can be issued.

(c) The buyer's department will know what arrangements have been made with the supplier.

(d) Desks'r'us should send a credit note for £200 (plus VAT) to Abacus when the desk is returned and an invoice for £200 (plus VAT) when the new desk is delivered.

Activity 3.3

Helping hand. Remember that gross labour costs include *all* payments made by an employer.

(a) The total labour cost for the two employees is made up of gross pay plus employer's contributions to pension and National Insurance. This comes to £3,383.11.

(b) The advisers should keep time sheets to record the time spent with clients.

(c) The charge per hour must cover overheads and profit as well as labour cost.

Activity 3.4

PAYROLL CALCULATION SCHEDULE APRIL 2001		
NAME:	Sandra Bloggs	
DEPARTMENT:	Denim Range	
BASIC RATE:	£6.00 per hour	
HOURS WORKED:	35	
HOURS FOR OVERTIME PREMIUM:	7	
	Calculation	**Amount** £
BASIC PAY	35 hrs × £6	210
OVERTIME PREMIUM	7 hrs × £6 × 0.5	21
EMPLOYER'S PENSION CONT	5% × £210	10.50
EMPLOYER'S NIC	£210 + £21 = £231 £231 – £84 = £147 £147 × 12.5%	18.37

Activity 3.5

Helping hand. Don't forget that VAT must be analysed and posted to the VAT account.

(a) The expenses shown are totals (including VAT) so VAT must be determined from the receipts, deducted from the expense totals and posted to the VAT account.

(b) For the training manager, both activities will count as training expenditure. For the saleswoman, the customer visit will be a sales cost but, according to company policy, the training course may be counted as part of either the sales or the training budget.

Activity 3.6

There are a number of possibilities. Entries to the record sheet may have an error (check the petty cash slips) or may have omitted a slip (is number 36 the last entry for April and has voucher 42 been used?). Someone may have 'borrowed' £2 from the tin (does anyone else have a key?) or the money may have been lost, for example, dropped on the floor.

Answer to Chapter 4 activities

Activity 4.1

This code would stand for ladies' red boots, size 4, style 10.

Activity 4.2

Telephone numbers and locations

		Code
020 7668 9923	Managing director	5510
020 7768 9871	Marketing manager	5530
020 7668 9893	Factory floor	5570
020 7668 9879	Accounts office	5510
00879 6534	Salesman's mobile	5530

Activity 4.3

Invoice no	*Net sales value* £	*Country*	*Code*
8730	10,360.00	Canada	R120
8731	12,750.73	Australia	R160
8732	5,640.39	Spain	R140
8733	15,530.10	Northern Ireland	R110
8734	3,765.75	South Africa	R150
8735	8,970.22	Kenya	R150
8736	11,820.45	Italy	R140
8737	7,640.00	France	R140
8738	9,560.60	Australia	R160
8739	16,750.85	Germany	R140

Activity 4.4

Helping hand. Proceeds of annual flag day could have arisen from a fundraising event or could have been donated to the charity. If you think more than one code might apply, don't be afraid to write them both down, giving your reasons.

(a) DO23
(b) TR17
(c) FR35
(d) GG10
(e) DO23 or possibly FR35 depending on policy
(f) GG10

Activity 4.5

(a) The purchase requisition might help by showing which department/person requested the goods.

(b) The research department and/or sales department might be able to help. Alternatively, an experienced person in your own department might know if the items are for resale or use by the research department.

(c) The research department or an experienced person in your own department should know.

(d) In many companies, invoices are 'passed for payment' by the person responsible for the expenditure. This person will know what the goods are for and could help by putting an explanatory note on the invoice.

Activity 4.6

(a) The audit, tax and corporate finance departments will deal with clients and therefore probably earn income.

(b) The general administration department will serve all three and is therefore likely to have its costs shared out between the other departments.

(c) The general administration department does not earn income and therefore cannot be a profit centre.

(d) It is most likely that if the firm is organised into different departments that earn different types of income that a separate revenue code will be created for each department (audit, tax and corporate finance).

Activity 4.7

(a) There are two problems which should be fairly obvious:

18/6 £230 seems an unlikely petrol bill

22/6 The purchase of a car has been coded to expenses instead of fixed assets

There are also bills for repairs, tyres and road tax all in one month which is probably not typical.

(b) (i) The petrol receipt should be checked and the entry corrected.

(ii) The entry for the purchase of the car should be corrected, ie removed from the expense account and re-entered under the appropriate fixed asset code.

(iii) No action is needed for the other motor expenses which are correctly coded.

Helping hand. Any items of expenditure on long-term fixed assets which a company intends to retain for its own use are capital items, not expense items.

Activity 4.8

CODING EXTRACT
INCOME AND EXPENDITURE
APRIL 2001

Code	Balance b/fwd 1.4.01	Amount coded April 2001	Balance at 30.04.01
	£	£	£
311	23,429	7,220	30,649
312	12,230	3,960	16,190
313	28,930	9,212	38,142
321	27,260	6,250	33,510
322	10,214	2,590	12,804
323	17,928	6,671	24,599
331	46,219	13,652	59,871
332	8,247	2,790	11,037
333	19,715	5,920	25,635
341	24,212	7,262	31,474
342	2,420	659	3,079
343	10,443	3,256	13,699

INCOME AND EXPENDITURE BALANCES YEAR TO DATE APRIL 2001	
Sales	**Balance at 30.04.01**
Denim Range	£
- UK	30,649
- Europe	33,510
- America	59,871
- Asia	31,474
Silk Range	
- UK	16,190
- Europe	12,804
- America	11,037
- Asia	3,079
Lycra Range	
- UK	38,142
- Europe	24,599
- America	25,635
- Asia	13,699

Answers to Chapter 5 activities

Activity 5.1

Helping hand. This question emphasises the most important qualities of management information; it must be **relevant** to the user and it must be **sufficient** for the user's needs.

There seem to be two problems here: too much budget information and not enough of any other type. Your questions should clarify what information can be left out of the current reports because it is irrelevant and what other information the user would like. Once you know what is wanted, for example numbers of customer complaints, time taken to reply to complaints etc, you will need to find out if this is already available or whether it can be collected in the future without undue expense.

Activity 5.2

Helping hand. At the top of the letter, remember to give the necessary details of the sender and recipient, including their references. As the letter is going to a named recipient it should be addressed to Mrs Wade and ended 'Yours sincerely'.

Brown Bros
24 Croxley Road
Coulton
Surrey
RH3 9BZ

Tel: 0192 730 1933
Fax: 0192 730 1934

Date: 11 May 2001
Our ref: ACF/pj

Your ref: LRS/NP

Mrs Susan Wade
Pebble and Sons
16 Rowe Street
Lambourn
Berks
MA6 3AJ

Dear Ms Wade,

Re: Your invoice 3452 dated 8 May 2001

Further to our telephone conversation today, this is to confirm that the agreed price for the 50 chairs on the above invoice was £20 per chair as per our order number 571, and not £25 as shown on your invoice.

Please issue us with a credit note to rectify this error.

Thank you for your help.

Yours sincerely

C Ford

Carol Ford
Accounts Supervisor

Activity 5.3

(a) A letter

(b) A memo, an e-mail (if available) or you could just ask face-to-face

(c) A formal report

(d) A standard letter

(e) An e-mail

(f) A memo, an e-mail, a telephone call or a face-to-face question.

Activity 5.4

Helping hand. This request appears to breach the requirements of the Data Protection Act since it is asking for 'sensitive' personal data. You must turn it down but need to do so tactfully.

MEMO

To:	Alan Jones (Marketing)	Date:	11.6.2001
From:	Jane Grey (Payroll)	Ref:	AJ/ads

Subject: Employee information

In reply to your memo of 10.6.2001. I regret to tell you that I cannot give you the information you have asked for. Under the Data Protection Act, we are required to keep this information confidential. I am sorry not to be more helpful and you may like to talk to the payroll supervisor (Pravina Tank, extension 7356) to see whether there is any way round this.

Activity 5.5

The fact that you do not have access to this information probably means it is subject to organisation policy on confidentiality. You could consult the organisation's policy manual for more information and should then ask your supervisor for further advice on what to do.

Answer to Chapter 6 activities

Activity 6.1

Helping hand. In (a) the information is not precise enough, in (b) you are not comparing like with like and in (c) other comparisons are needed.

(a) Daily figures will not help the foreman to judge the performance of his particular shift (there are other shifts during the day).

(b) You would expect December sales to be the highest for the year so comparison with December last year and the year-to-date with last year might be more meaningful.

(c) Exam results only measure one aspect of a school's objectives and will be affected by the quality of pupils as well as teachers.

Activity 6.2

Helping hand. In (b) you need to quantify why the differences arose.

(a) Actual sales revenue could be found in the ledger accounts for sales.

(b) Sales Revenue Report April to June

April		*May*		*June*		*Total*	
Actual	Budgeted	Actual	Budgeted	Actual	Budgeted	Actual	Budgeted
£'000	£'000	£'000	£'000	£'000	£'000	£'000	£'000
9.0	8.8	10.2	9.6	11.8	11.9	31.0	30.3

Note

Sales revenue for the 3 months is £700 more than budgeted.

In April, the quantity sold was greater than budget resulting in £200 revenue over budget. In May, a price rise of 50p per gallon (not in the budget until June) resulted in an increase in revenue of £600 over budget although the amount sold was as planned. In June, the quantity sold was under budget resulting in a £100 revenue shortfall.

Activity 6.3

Helping hand. The key to this activity is determining who makes the decisions about which costs.

(a) Nursing salaries would probably be centrally controlled by the hospital and influenced by NHS salaries. Drugs would be determined by a doctor and administered by a nurse. Dressings are probably the only item the ward sister has any control over.

(b) The £300 drugs cost for March looks quite different from the normal pattern of cost. You should look at the ledger account and purchase documents to see if it is correct.

(c) Combining drugs and dressings costs does not seem helpful in a ward report since only one is a controllable cost for the ward sister.

Activity 6.4

Helping hand. Using % increase may result in small £ changes being highlighted (if budgeted cost is £1, actual cost is £3, the variance is 200%). However % variances may be a good guide to problems with the assumptions behind budgets.

(a)

	Budgeted	Actual	Variance	Variance
	£	£	£	%
Laundry	1,000	1,045	45(A)	4.5
Heat and light	1,500	1,420	80(F)	5.3
Catering	8,500	8,895	395(A)	4.6
Nursing staff	7,000	6,400	600(F)	8.6
Ancillary staff	10,600	10,950	350(A)	3.3

$$\text{Variance \%} = \frac{\text{Actual costs} - \text{Budgeted costs}}{\text{Budgeted costs}} \times 100\%$$

(b) Only the cost of nursing staff

(c) Heat and light and nursing staff

Activity 6.5

Helping hand. This illustrates not only the importance of non-financial objectives, but also how failure to meet non-financial objectives may impact upon financial objectives.

This is only good if the necessary standards of cleanliness can be maintained. If they can be, then there were probably too many cleaners before. If standards fall, there will be other effects (like more patient infections) which will cost more in the long term and damage the chief goal of improving health.

Activity 6.6

Helping hand. Note that the action to control the variance may be needed by Brown or the manager.

(a)

Variances	*Month 4*	*YTD*
Green	£500 (favourable)	£5,000 (favourable)
Brown	£400 (adverse)	£5,000 (adverse)

(b) The variances may be controllable. The manager needs to find out why Brown is below target. If he has been sick or on holiday, he may need to make more calls in the next few months. However, he may need more training or greater incentives; if so the manager should try to provide what he needs.

(c) The action taken depends on the reasons for both variances. Total sales for the regions are as planned for the year so far, so there is no effect on the production plan. The manager should assess whether Brown is really underperforming (see part (b)). Alternatively Brown may have more 'difficult' customers than Green. If so, the manager should consider changing targets or swapping some customers between the two salesmen.

Activity 6.7

Helping hand. Another illustration of the importance of non-financial objectives.

(a) The suggestions miss the point that the library does not seem to be meeting the needs of staff and students. Until this is remedied, there is no point (and probably no chance) of taking over staff stocks. Using information staff for cataloguing is not likely to improve library service either.

(b) Library performance cannot be measured only in terms of money since low spending might mean that staff books, facilities etc are insufficient rather than that it is efficiently run.

(c) Other measures should reflect the goals of the library service. These could include levels of usage (perhaps analysed by department), surveys of customer satisfaction, new books purchased, numbers of enquiries dealt with etc.

Activity 6.8

Helping hand. In answering activities such as (a), you need to think about how what one department does can affect another. In (b) quantities sold might also be important as well as sales revenue. A decrease in quantity may imply that the business's share of the market has decreased.

(a) The fact that sales are less in quantity than expected will affect the department which store stock (there will be more!) and/or the production department (they may have to revise their plans and make less).

(b) Although the quantity sold is below budget, the sales revenue is more than budget. Whether or not the sales manager gets his bonus will depend on how the company defines 'successful' for this purpose.

Activity 6.9

VARIANCE REPORT
PRODUCTION COST CENTRES
APRIL 2001

	Year to 30 April 2001
	£
Materials	4,038 (A)
Labour	4,022 (A)
Expenses	3,781 (A)

Comment

The significant variances which are more than 10% from budget are:

- Materials £4,038 (A) = 11.5%
- Expenses £3,781 (A) = 25.2%

Answers to Chapter 7 activities

Activity 7.1

Helping hand. In (a) the difference between the original net profit (£10,000) and the net loss of B is dropped (£40,000) is £50,000, the contribution of B.

B's contribution = Sales revenue – Variable costs
= £70,000 – £20,000
= £50,000

In (b) note that there are a number of different options. The point in (iv) about the allocation of fixed costs is something we can only mention briefly here, but you will study the issues in depth at Intermediate level.

(a) If Product B is dropped, its variable costs (£70,000) will be saved but the fixed costs will still have to be paid.

	Product A
	£'000
Sales revenue	100
Less: Direct costs	(40)
Less: Fixed product overheads	(40)
Gross profit	20
Less: Other fixed costs	(60)
Net loss	(40)

(b) The company could

(i) Use the spare capacity freed by not producing Product B to make more of Product A
(ii) Investigate the possibility of using the spare capacity to make a new Product
(iii) Raise the price of Product B
(iv) Investigate the way fixed costs have been shared between the two products

Activity 7.2

Helping hand. (d) introduces the idea that there is more to pricing decisions than purely mathematical calculations.

(a) Each can contributes 10p (40p – 30p) to fixed costs.

(b) It must sell 500,000 cans to cover fixed costs (£50,000 divided by 10p).

(c) Budgeted profit will be £25,000 = (750,000 × 10p) – £50,000 (fixed costs).

(d) If there is spare capacity in the factory then this order will contribute an extra £1,000 to profits (20,000 × contribution of 5p). It might, however upset regular customers if they got to hear of it.

Activity 7.3

Helping hand. Note the following features about the report.

(a) An introduction and terms of reference
(b) Stating of assumptions (using the sales manager's forecasts)
(c) Report divided into clearly headed sections
(d) Clear conclusions with a recommended course of action

The report considers the purchase cost issue separately from maintenance. Note that the costs of one option (purchasing outright and not taking out a maintenance contract) are uncertain; risk is therefore involved in the decision.

Cash flow may also be important. Even if immediate purchase is significantly cheaper ultimately than the other options, it will still be too expensive if you cannot come up with the money now!

The report might look something like this.

FEASIBILITY REPORT FOR OFFICE DRINKS VENDING MACHINE

Terms of reference

1 To determine whether forecast sales will cover costs
2 To compare the benefits of purchase or leasing
3 To identify any other issues which need consideration

Introduction

1 This report was requested by the office manager
2 I have used her forecasts of selling prices and sales
3 Other information comes from the supplier's literature
4 My cost comparisons are made over 5 years

1 **Will forecast cover sales?**

Both coffee and tea are to be sold at 30p per cup. Coffee costs 22p per cup and tea 20p per cup. Forecast sales are 17,000 cups of coffee and 11,000 cups of tea per year.

	Coffee	*Tea*	*Total*
	£	£	£
Revenue	5,100	3,300	8,400
Less Variable costs	3,740	2,200	5,940
Contribution per year	1,360	1,100	2,460

A 5-year lease on the machine would cost £780 a year which would easily be covered. The total lease cost over 5 years would be £3,900.

Purchase of the machine would be £2,600 and would be covered in just over one year

2 **Maintenance**

Under the leasing contract, maintenance would be undertaken by the supplier so the total cost of £3,900 over five years is not affected by maintenance costs.

Outright purchase could be combined with a maintenance contract at £150 a year. This would bring the total cost over five years to £3,350.

Alternatively, we could call in a repairer as necessary but, since the cost is unknown, this would be a more risky option.

3 **Cash flow considerations**

Outright purchase of the machine, although cheaper in total, requires a larger outlay at the outset. The leasing contract would spread the outlay more evenly over the five years.

Conclusions

1 On forecast sales, the costs of the machine is easily covered whichever option is chosen.

2 Outright purchase without a maintenance contract is the cheapest but most risky option and puts the most pressure on immediate cash resources.

3 Adding the maintenance contract to purchase reduces the risk and is still cheaper than leasing.

4 The main benefit of leasing is to spread the cost evenly.

Recommendation

I recommend purchase of the machine and the annual maintenance contract

Susan Scott

....

Activity 7.4

Helping hand. Fixed costs need not be included in the calculations for pricing in this example. They remain the same whatever price is charged, that is they are not relevant to this decision. You will still get the same answer if you do include them, but it is quicker just to look at the contribution.

The price options will give the following results.

Sales volume	Price per unit	Variable cost per unit	Contribution	
			Per unit	Total
Units	£	£	£	£
29,000	4.00	2.20	1.80	52,200
25,000	4.50	2.20	2.30	57,500
20,000	5.00	2.20	2.80	56,000
17,000	5.50	2.20	3.30	56,100
15,000	6.00	2.20	3.80	57,000

A price of £4.50 will therefore give the highest profit.

If £6,000 is spent on advertising, then an extra 10% of sales can be achieved at this price.

This will only increase total contribution by 10% (£5,750) and is therefore not worth doing.

List of key terms and index

These are the terms which we have identified throughtout the text as being KEY TERMS. You should make sure that you can define what these terms mean; go back to the pages highlighted here if you need to check.

ORDER FORM

Any books from our AAT range can be ordered by telephoning 020 8740 2211. Alternatively, send this page to our address below, fax it to us on 020 8740 1184, or email us at **publishing@bpp.com.** Or look us up on our website: www.bpp.com

We aim to deliver to all UK addresses inside 5 working days; a signature will be required. Orders to all EU addresses should be delivered within 6 working days. All other orders to overseas addresses should be delivered within 8 working days.

To: BPP Publishing Ltd, Aldine House, Aldine Place, London W12 8AW

Tel: 020-8740 2211 **Fax: 020-8740 1184** **Email: publishing@bpp.com**

Mr / Ms (full name): ______________________

Daytime delivery address: ______________________

____

Postcode: ______________ Daytime Tel: ______________

Please send me the following quantities of books.

	5/01 Interactive Text	8/01 DA Kit	8/01 Combined Kit	8/01 CA Kit
FOUNDATION				
Unit 1 Recording Income and Receipts (6/01 Kit)	☐	☐		
Unit 2 Making and Recording Payments (6/01 Kit)	☐	☐		
Unit 3 Ledger Balances and Initial Trial Balance (6/01 Kit)	☐		☐	
Unit 4 Supplying Information for Management Control (6/01 Kit)	☐	☐		
Unit 20 Working with Information Technology (8/01 Text)	☐			
Unit 22/23 Healthy Workplace and Personal Effectiveness	☐			
INTERMEDIATE				
Unit 5 Financial Records and Accounts	☐		☐	
Unit 6 Cost Information	☐		☐	
Unit 7 Reports and Returns	☐	☐		
Unit 21 Using Information Technology	☐	☐		
TECHNICIAN				
Unit 8/9 Core Managing Costs and Allocating Resources	☐			☐
Unit 10 Core Managing Accounting Systems	☐	☐		
Unit 11 Option Financial Statements (Accounting Practice)	☐			☐
Unit 12 Option Financial Statements (Central Government)	☐			☐
Unit 15 Option Cash Management and Credit Control	☐	☐		
Unit 16 Option Evaluating Activities	☐	☐		
Unit 17 Option Implementing Auditing Procedures	☐	☐		
Unit 18 Option Business Tax FA01(8/01 Text)	☐	☐		
Unit 19 Option Personal Tax FA01(8/01 Text)	☐	☐		
TECHNICIAN 2000				
Unit 18 Option Business Tax FA00 (8/00 Text & Kit)	☐	☐		
Unit 19 Option Personal Tax FA00 (8/00 Text & Kit)	☐	☐		
TOTAL BOOKS	☐ +	☐ +	☐ +	☐ = ☐

@ £9.95 each = £

Special offer

Foundation units £80 complete set £

Intermediate units £65 complete set £

Technician units £100 complete set £

Postage and packaging

UK: £2.00 for each book to maximum of £10

Europe (inc ROI and Channel Islands): £4.00 for first book, £2.00 for each extra

Rest of the World: £20.00 for first book, £10 for each extra

P & P £

GRAND TOTAL £

I enclose a cheque for £ _________ (cheques to BPP Publishing Ltd) or charge to Mastercard/Visa/Switch

Card number ☐☐☐☐☐☐☐☐☐☐☐☐☐☐☐☐☐☐☐

Start date ______________ **Expiry date** ______________ **Issue no. (Switch only)**______

Signature ______________________

REVIEW FORM & FREE PRIZE DRAW

All original review forms from the entire BPP range, completed with genuine comments, will be entered into one of two draws on 31 January 2002 and 31 July 2002. The names on the first four forms picked out on each occasion will be sent a cheque for £50.

Name: ______________________ **Address:** ______________________

____

____

How have you used this Interactive Text? *(Tick one box only)*

- ☐ Home study (book only)
- ☐ On a course: college ______________
- ☐ With 'correspondence' package
- ☐ Other ______________

Why did you decide to purchase this Interactive Text? *(Tick one box only)*

- ☐ Have used BPP Texts in the past
- ☐ Recommendation by friend/colleague
- ☐ Recommendation by a lecturer at college
- ☐ Saw advertising
- ☐ Other ______________

During the past six months do you recall seeing/receiving any of the following? *(Tick as many boxes as are relevant)*

- ☐ Our advertisement in *Accounting Technician* magazine
- ☐ Our advertisement in *Pass*
- ☐ Our brochure with a letter through the post

Which (if any) aspects of our advertising do you find useful? *(Tick as many boxes as are relevant)*

- ☐ Prices and publication dates of new editions
- ☐ Information on Interactive Text content
- ☐ Facility to order books off-the-page
- ☐ None of the above

Have you used the companion Assessment Kit for this subject? ☐ **Yes** ☐ **No**

Your ratings, comments and suggestions would be appreciated on the following areas

	Very useful	*Useful*	*Not useful*
Introductory section (How to use this Interactive Text etc)	☐	☐	☐
Chapter topic lists	☐	☐	☐
Chapter learning objectives	☐	☐	☐
Key terms	☐	☐	☐
Assessment alerts	☐	☐	☐
Examples	☐	☐	☐
Activities and answers	☐	☐	☐
Key learning points	☐	☐	☐
Quick quizzes and answers	☐	☐	☐
List of key terms and index	☐	☐	☐
Icons	☐	☐	☐

	Excellent	*Good*	*Adequate*	*Poor*
Overall opinion of this Text	☐	☐	☐	☐

Do you intend to continue using BPP Interactive Texts/Assessment Kits? ☐ Yes ☐ No

Please note any further comments and suggestions/errors on the reverse of this page.

Please return to: Nick Weller, BPP Publishing Ltd, FREEPOST, London, W12 8BR

REVIEW FORM & FREE PRIZE DRAW (continued)

Please note any further comments and suggestions/errors below

FREE PRIZE DRAW RULES

1 Closing date for 31 January 2002 draw is 31 December 2001. Closing date for 31 July 2002 draw is 30 June 2002.

2 Restricted to entries with UK and Eire addresses only. BPP employees, their families and business associates are excluded.

3 No purchase necessary. Entry forms are available upon request from BPP Publishing. No more than one entry per title, per person. Draw restricted to persons aged 16 and over.

4 Winners will be notified by post and receive their cheques not later than 6 weeks after the relevant draw date.

5 The decision of the promoter in all matters is final and binding. No correspondence will be entered into.